MAGICAL REALISM
FOR NON-BELIEVERS

MAGICAL

REALISM

FOR

NON-BELIEVERS

A MEMOIR OF
FINDING FAMILY

ANIKA FAJARDO

UNIVERSITY OF MINNESOTA PRESS
MINNEAPOLIS ▪ LONDON

Published by the University of Minnesota Press
111 Third Avenue South, Suite 290
Minneapolis, MN 55401-2520
http://www.upress.umn.edu

Printed in the United States of America on acid-free paper

The University of Minnesota is an equal-opportunity educator and employer.

24 23 22 21 20 19   10 9 8 7 6 5 4 3 2 1

Library of Congress Cataloging-in-Publication Data
Fajardo, Anika, author.
Magical realism for non-believers : a memoir of finding family / Anika Fajardo.
Minneapolis : University of Minnesota Press, [2019]
Identifiers: LCCN 2018037433 (print) | ISBN 978-1-5179-0686-3 (hc/j)
Subjects: LCSH: Fajardo, Anika. | Fajardo, Anika—Family. | Colombian
  Americans—Minnesota—Minneapolis—Biography. | Minneapolis
  (Minn.)—Biography. | Colombia—Biography.
Classification: LCC F614.M553 F34 2019 (print) | DDC 977.6/579053—dc23
LC record available at https://lccn.loc.gov/2018037433

TO DAVE

PROLOGUE

WHEN I ARRIVED IN COLOMBIA, my father hugged me and kissed me as if we had done this before, as if we were family, as if we had not been apart for a lifetime. I remember the damp night air as I stepped through the whir of automatic doors from the antiseptic white of the terminal into the suffocating heat. Santiago de Cali, the capital city of the Valle de Cauca province, is only three hundred miles from the equator, and the tropical heat caught in my throat with its sweet pungency of exotic fruits and diesel exhaust. I remember hearing my name, a shout above the chorus of *gritos*. I looked up and saw a face that was eerily familiar.

Even though two decades had lapsed since the pictures I had of him were taken, I could still identify this man. My father. Renzo. His black hair and mustache, now threaded with strands of gray, were recognizable from the yellowed snapshots. His high cheekbones (the ones I had inherited) looked like they must have at some point left a certain type of woman swooning. He wore thick, dark-rimmed glasses, and I suspected that the fine lines behind the lenses had come from years of winking at pretty girls. "Renzo was so handsome," my mother used to gush—literally gush—and I tried to see in him what she had seen. But I could only compare his seemingly instantaneous aging (that transition from a young husband in old photographs to this graying man in real life) to that of my mother, whom I had watched throughout my life, day by day, and whose soft lines and fading hair were imperceptible to me.

"Hello," he said with a strong emphasis on the *h* as if it would get away if he didn't catch it in his mouth. He was, I should have seen then, a master of understatement, a magician with unassuming gestures and kept secrets. This greeting in English seemed somehow hollow, falling short of expectation. Where were the Spanish flourishes to mark the occasion of a father meeting his adult daughter? But maybe he didn't know what to say. What do you say to someone who is kin and yet not, who shares your DNA but about whom you know nothing? *Hello* was perhaps the only option.

He put his brown hand on the shoulder of a young and solid-looking woman next to him. "This is my wife, María Cecilia—Ceci," he said, and I kissed them both in greeting from across the barricade before making my way around the mass of Colombians, who greeted one another with the enthusiasm and abandon that I recognized as the missing ingredient in our first exchange.

But when at last I had made it past the throngs of passengers and luggage, when no physical barrier was between us, he hugged me, squeezed me until my neck was cramped into an unnatural angle. He smelled of cigarette smoke and soap, and the wiry hairs of his mustache tickled my cheek. It felt strange to hug a man so small, no taller than my mother. When he embraced me—as if physical closeness could spawn intimacy—I held on, hoping and wondering if he was right.

Ceci, cute and compact in a short sundress and thong sandals, hugged me, too. Her shoulder-length hair was pulled into an unruly ponytail and outlined her smooth, brown face. In an accent so thick I almost didn't understand her, she greeted me enthusiastically in English.

As I followed this man and his wife to their car, a foreign-sounding bird cried from the trees at the edge of the parking lot. I couldn't help thinking of Macondo, the fictional village in *One Hundred Years of Solitude,* the town that had been formed by hacking away the vegetation of the jungle to make way for the Buendía family. I had read Gabriel García Márquez's novel when I was in high school, and even while I was reading it, I had felt the weight of expectation that I should love the book because it was Colombian. Like the assumptions that I should prefer spicy foods and tan easily, it felt as if I should love everything

Colombian because of my birthplace. And while I couldn't tolerate hot chilis and my shoulders did occasionally burn on bright summer days, I had wanted to love the novel simply because I had wanted Colombia to prove to me how beautiful, magical, wonderful she was, to show me why my father had chosen her over me.

"You sit in front," my father said, climbing into the back of a tiny Suzuki jeep, which smelled of bananas and warm summer days. It was nine in the evening, and as Ceci honked and lurched around slow-moving cars and crowded roundabouts, I wondered if Colombia would always be for me a jostling and jerking of motion and movement, a stretching and folding of moments and minutes.

I watched children—barely tall enough to peek inside—pester us at every red light, asking to wash the windows or sell us bags of unfamiliar fruit. I had not yet tasted the sweetness of the *guyaba* and *guanábana* and *maracuyá*. From the car I watched a black woman in a colorful turban selling something out of a basket that rested between her ample knees. "¡Chontaduros!" she called. Later I learned that I didn't like this small, hard fruit cooked with salt—not everything in Colombia met my expectations or satisfied my palate. Young men on bicycles wove in and out among tiny cars and speeding traffic, oblivious to danger. Strung between turquoise and salmon buildings, white shirts and blue towels fluttered like flags. The lights of the houses on the hills surrounding Cali twinkled in the night and looked like stars.

1

WHEN MY MOTHER FIRST ARRIVED IN COLOMBIA, she was nineteen, just a bit younger than I was now. I tried to imagine her seeing this place for the first time. For the tenth time. Did she get used to it? Did the things she saw eventually become just part of the landscape, or did they remain foreign? I tried to fit it all into what I had imagined, the man seated behind me into the shape of a father.

Ceci drove and gesticulated, and my father leaned between the seats. "Are you hungry?" he asked. "¿Qué quieres comer?"

I didn't know what I wanted to eat. I was barely off the airplane, still transitioning. My last meal had been something with rubbery chicken and atrophied mushrooms on flight 965, the same number of the American Airlines flight bound for Colombia that had, just one week earlier, landed not on the runway of the Alfonso Aragón International Airport but nose first in the mountains surrounding the city. The village of Buga was the deathbed for most of the nearly sixty people aboard the 757. My father told me later that his friend was in the village at the time and watched looters search for cash left in singed wallets and valuables hidden in dented suitcases. As news of the crash made its way around the world that day, I was in the kitchen of my mother's little bungalow in Minneapolis, the one she bought after her second divorce. I was packing for the month between college semesters that I would spend in Colombia.

"I'm so afraid," I had told my mother from across the red linoleum, gritty with spilled sugar from Christmas baking. Fear had rippled through me and around me, infested its way inside the winter layers I wore, and bored into the vertebrae of my spine, the tendons between my toes, the soft palate beneath my tongue. I could feel every molecule of my body urging me: don't go.

"I know," said my mother, who too had been alone when she traveled to Colombia as a young woman. She had probably been afraid, too, but her fear must have been a reflection of her sheltered upbringing and shy tendencies. She had gone for adventure, a semester abroad, a new experience; we both knew I had more to fear.

When she sank into a creaky kitchen chair, I collapsed into her, weeping. She held me on her lap like a baby. "You don't have to go if you don't want to."

But I had to, I needed to. And one week later I found myself pressed into my seat by the acceleration of takeoff, my entire body feeling the preposterousness of air travel. When we were at last miraculously airborne, a man across the aisle leaned toward me. He had black hair and wore a button-down shirt over a stomach that was just beginning to paunch. He smiled and asked in better English than my Spanish, "Are you visiting family?"

Family to me meant my mother's little bungalow in Minneapolis, it meant a log cabin built by my grandparents on the edge of a lake in Minnesota, it meant uncles and cousins and friends who occasionally entered my trajectory. Could it also mean strangers in Colombia?

"I'm visiting my father," I told the man, the simplest answer.

"Do you visit him every Christmas?"

I shook my head. "I've never met him before," I said. I don't know what I expected from this explanation, this story I had told before. The story of my not knowing my own father. Like anyone's life history, it is both intensely personal and yet in some way, acutely universal.

The man nodded and told me that his wife's daughter was also half-Colombian, that she had never met her father either.

"Well, I was born there," I felt the need to clarify, as if differentiating myself from what, apparently, was an epidemic of unknown and unmet Colombian fathers. As much as I wanted to fit in, I also wanted my unique story to be heard. "I just don't remember him," I added.

But I wondered how different knowing and remembering were. I met countless people whose names I immediately forgot, I remembered stories that never happened, and I knew nothing about ones that had.

Maybe, I thought as Ceci and my father exchanged mumbled, incomprehensible words while we were stopped at a red light, I would discover which was which. "My dear," my father said, laying a hand on my shoulder. "We'll eat at Crepes y Waffles."

I don't think the crepes and waffles chain was around in the early 1970s when my parents lived together in Colombia. Maybe their marriage would have survived if it had been, if my mother could have ordered fast-food sweets. Colombia was more foreign then than it is now, and I wonder if globalization could have saved my parents' marriage.

My mother had told me about the salty, cheese-filled *arepas* you could buy on the street corners and the deep bowls of *sancocho* that accompanied every family gathering. She told me about her mother-in-law's black beans and tamales.

"Doña Rosa made the best tamales," she would tell me. "They're different from Mexican ones."

When I was growing up in Minnesota with my Minnesotan mother, Mexican food was the closest I had come to experiencing South American cuisine. She had served tacos with store-bought shells and sour cream, and we ate mild enchilada casseroles. For school reports about my birth country, my mother would help me make the laborious *manjar blanco,* and I remember the sweet, slightly burnt taste of the caramel-like Colombian dessert.

Ceci pulled into a dirt parking lot, where teenagers and families loitered in the warm evening. The long wooden tables on the cement patio were crowded, and a menu was painted on the bright orange wall of the building. The strains of "Angels We Have Heard on High" playing through tinny loudspeakers reminded me of the Christmas Eve I had just spent with my mother and grandparents a few days before. I watched the white lightbulbs swing from wires above us and blot out the stars. This wasn't anything like the Colombia my mother had described.

We found seats at a wobbly wooden table, Ceci talking and my father smiling. Twenty years had lapsed since the pictures I have of him were taken, and although he still wore a mustache, he was shorter and looked older than I thought he would.

"Ay, Renzo, que chévere, la familia acá juntos." Ceci smiled at both of us. She looked much younger than my father, and I later learned that she had been his student in a photography class. My mother had been my father's student for a time also, making me wonder about the cycles and circles we are bound to repeat.

"Hay que estar cansadita después del vuelo y tanto viaje. ¿A dónde vamos mañana por la mañana?" She talked, and her words were like a machine gun's rat-a-tat-tat. I struggled to understand and clung to anything I recognized: *Family. Happy. Welcome.*

She turned to the menu and then to me. "¿Qué quieres?"

What did I want? The last time I had eaten crepes they were broccoli-stuffed buckwheat ones made by my mother. She had fed me, her only child, on whole grains and garden vegetables; she had cooked with an agenda of health and economy. I looked at the menu and didn't know what I wanted.

The crepe Ceci ordered for me was decidedly not buckwheat. It was rich and sweet, filled with vanilla ice cream, a few plump strawberries, and smothered in thick whipped cream. The only relief from the tooth-aching sweetness was the delicate, light pancake. As I washed down each bite with sips of warm Coke, I thought about my mother's crepes. I thought about Doña Rosa's tamales and whether I would get to try *arepas*. I wondered what my mother would say one month from now when I told her my first Colombian meal was crepes.

"¿Te gusta, no?" Ceci asked, grinning.

I looked at the two strangers sitting opposite me and nodded. I did like it.

■ ■ ■

There is a photograph of my mother from the early 1970s. She is framed by a window, her back to a Colombian cityscape. Vertical stripes of orange and white and brown decorate her hip-huggers, match her brown blouse. A shank of dishwater-blonde hair shades one eye, and her head is at an angle as if she is about to brush her hair out of her face with one casual move. She's smiling in what was perhaps only a brief and fleeting feeling of contentment, no hint of the heartache to come. Photographs hold their subjects frozen in time, the only indication of passing years the yellowing of the colors and the softening of the paper. In real life, time marches onward, changing and transforming us.

In an age before constant social media updates, my father had no idea what to expect from me when I arrived. Did he imagine that I would be slender and blonde like my mother had been? Did he picture me in a sundress and thong sandals like Ceci? In the airplane, I had watched the passengers become increasingly jubilant, effervescent, expansive. Spanish had bombarded me from all sides, buffeting and jostling me even more than the turbulence. As the collective mood rose, a parade of women tipped and swayed down the aisle toward the bathroom. In what looked like a practiced ritual, they went in wearing jeans and sweaters, shorts, and running shoes and emerged from the tiny closets like butterflies, their shirts and pants replaced with halter-neck sundresses patterned like jungle oases, with low-cut blouses and miniskirts, with spiky heels and open-toed sandals. Tired faces were redrawn with sun-kissed rouge and black eyeliner, smiles refreshed with crimson lipstick. I stumbled off the plane still cocooned in winter's thick wool and my baggy, misshapen jeans.

My very appearance—my actual being—was a marker for both my foreignness and artlessness, pointing out all the ways I didn't belong. If I were to be kind to my twenty-one-year-old self, I would cut myself some slack for arriving in clunky Doc Martens, baggy Levis, and unflattering bobbed hair. After all, in 1995 the world was less connected than it is now with its instantaneous communication capabilities and 24/7 news cycle, and I had no way of knowing that Seattle's grunge look hadn't penetrated South America.

That first morning, even before we left the hot valley city of Cali, even before we drove to his hometown of Popayán ninety miles to the south, my father and Ceci took me to buy new jeans. The low-altitude heat hung thick, and the sun beat down as Ceci zipped through traffic-clogged streets. She pulled up on a sidewalk next to a shop with open, glassless windows. Yanking the Suzuki into first gear, she climbed out and walked in ahead of me. The small space was lined from floor to ceiling with denim meant to lengthen the leg or accent a round behind. Even with open windows, the stench of sweatshop fabric and harsh cleaning products pummeled me. Instead of following us into the shop, my father chose that moment to stand on the sidewalk with a cigarette, leaving me at the mercy of Colombian fashion, an abandonment that felt almost like the one twenty years earlier.

"Tiene mucho culo," Ceci had announced to the saleslady who approached us. A big ass.

My mother had been shocked, she told me, by the frankness of the sexual tension in the air, the whistles and catcalls, when she first arrived in Colombia. "Ven acá, mamita," the dark strangers called salaciously to her from car windows and on street corners. My mother had tugged at her shorts that suddenly felt too short. During that first semester in Colombia, she had stayed in a rooming house in Cali, where the proprietress looked after her and the other college girls like daughters. The only other tenants were two black-clad phantoms, old ladies who covered their heads in tight black scarves that accentuated the deep creases of their faces. My mother told me that the spinsters would tell them, *What beautiful skin you girls have.* And my mother had been startled by the compliment, had run a hand along her cheek. In Minnesota she hadn't attracted that kind of notice; here she found that her accent and her pale skin made her desirable and charming.

That I had *mucho culo* was, of course, no surprise to me, having carried around this ass my whole life. In ballet class when I was seven, the old white man who taught little girls pliés and chassés kept telling me to tuck in my tush. But I never could. It always sat out there by itself, and, having grown up surrounded by flat-bottomed Swedes and Germans, I could only assume that this was a bad thing.

The saleslady, as if especially chosen to make me feel even more insecure, was petite but curvy in all the right places. She wore thick lipstick and chortled conspiratorially as she grabbed piles of jeans. Through the gap in the fitting room's curtain, I could see Ceci absently inspecting the styles as she waited. I hated jeans, I thought as I pulled on the first pair, yanking on the belt loops to get the jeans past my hips. That day, still groggy with jet lag and culture shock, I studied my reflection in the mirror and saw only imperfections: the ill-fitting pants, the shadow of a pimple about to emerge, the teeth that were too far apart, the bushy eyebrows.

At last a pair of jeans glided up with only a little tugging, and I emerged from the dressing room to get Ceci's approval. She made a catcall whistle. The denim flaunted my ass and thighs in a way that reminded me of the sundress I wore for my role as bridesmaid for my mother's second wedding. The dress was white cotton with a plunging décolletage that worried my mother. "In Shakespeare's day," my grandmother had assured her, "girls always showed off their breasts."

All the same, I had been barely fourteen, and my mother bought me a pink tank top to wear beneath the dress and provide a little modesty. Even with the extra layer, I remember feeling exposed. I had been acutely aware of the scooped neckline as I followed my mother down the makeshift aisle in the backyard, as I watched her giggling during the exchange of rings (which I knew, even then, to be a bad omen). After the ceremony, there was a pool party in the yard, and everyone changed into swimming suits. My mother's new husband got drunker and drunker, sank deeper and deeper into his inner tube in the pool until he was a mirage, an illusion of a happy groom. My uncles had hauled him out of the pool and put him to bed, and I never really liked the white dress after that. I wished it wasn't so white, so revealing.

"A ver," said Ceci, standing back to examine me.

The jeans did not transform me, but in the shop's large mirror

I looked less pale, and my cheeks, perhaps from the effort of trying on jeans, had flushed pink in an attractive way. From this distance I couldn't make out the pimple, and while I listened to Ceci and the saleslady, my mouth was closed, the gap in my teeth invisible. The inseam was too long, but the saleslady folded them under at the ankles, using the same technique that the cosmopolitan Spaniards had employed. I remembered my last day in Spain, when the taxi driver had mistaken me for a native.

"¿A dónde se va? Where are you headed?" he had asked.

"I'm taking the train to Madrid," I answered in Spanish.

"Are you going home for the summer?"

I looked at him in the rearview mirror. "What?" I asked in my hard-earned Castilian.

"Does your family live in Madrid?"

I loosened the scarf around my neck, the one I had bought at Zara in Valladolid a few months earlier after admiring the scarves on the Spanish women. The taxi driver thought I was a Spaniard, I had recognized. After six months of studying not only the language but also the way the women walked and talked, the way they asked "¿Tienes fuego?" when they needed a light for their cigarettes, I finally fit in.

And if I could do that in Spain, I thought, standing in front of the mirror, I surely could do it in Colombia, in the country where I had actually been born.

"Perfecto," the saleslady announced, stepping back to admire her work.

I remember Ceci inspecting me. "Mejor," she said. Better.

My father lived on the outskirts of Popayán, a city in the Andes in southern Colombia. The house was in a middle-class subdivision along the Pan-American Highway called Campo Bello, which I translated as "beautiful country." Beyond the borders of Campo Bello was open pastureland where white and gray cows grazed, the long flaps of skin under their chins waggling and their udders bulging. Single-family homes lined the unpaved streets at uneven intervals since not all the lots had been sold yet.

My father's was an elegant house with electricity, hot water, cable television. Part house, part fortress, it was surrounded by tall brick walls topped with broken bottles. In a land of drug cartels and right-wing radicals, these walls must have given the home a certain kind of rudimentary protection. Anyone attempting to scale the twenty-foot barrier would be met at the top with jagged glass that would cut the palms and leave a trickle of telltale blood. Just in case the walls didn't do the trick, each night of my stay I watched Ceci line up empty beer bottles at the threshold of the front door to be knocked over by possible intruders. I never asked, but I wanted to know who kept vigil at night, who listened for the crash of glass bottles on tile floors, and what they would do about it. I wanted to know how they protected themselves.

In the 1970s and 1980s, attempts at peace and reconciliation were made by the Colombian government and other factions, but in the 1990s, kidnappings increased, and Marxist guerillas roamed the countryside. By the time of my arrival in December 1995, Colombia was one of the most dangerous countries on Earth. The U.S. State Department warned against visits, and I was injected with all manner of vaccinations before departing. But my father, like all his neighbors, must have grown used to the extra precautions; they must have had a supernatural ability to keep an eye on peripheries; they must have learned not to jump at the sound of a backfiring car and not to wonder if it was a bomb. Even though sometimes it must have been.

A half century of violence and unrest had turned a beautiful country into bloody headlines and marginalized political policy. I don't know if my mother ever worried about the civil war that raged even during her time in Colombia or if she was too young, too naive, too invincible. She never told me. Instead, she told me about the warm friends and gracious neighbors and also about the unruly and crude boys in the English classes she taught. She talked about her mother-in-law's delicious tamales, but she also told me how *los suegros* had their own key to the apartment in Popayán and would arrive unannounced. With in-laws of my own now, I cringe at the thought. My mother told me about the beauty of Colombia but was also quick to point out its idiosyncrasies, inconveniences, and irritants. The unspoken one being my father.

My parents—before they were my parents—lived in a string of apartments and rented houses with varying levels of modern conveniences: the basement of my grandparents' house in Minnesota, the apartment in Cali, the walk-up duplex in Minneapolis, and the haunted house in Popayán. They lived with hand-me-down furniture and cockroaches, they hung weavings and sketches on their walls, they walked down the block to use a pay phone. The 1970s were a time when many people perfected the art of going with the flow, and perhaps my mother watched it all with the detached observance of an outsider. And she was young and in love. Love lets you overlook many shortcomings.

"Would you like to unpack?" my father asked, opening the closet and taking out an old-fashioned luggage stand. He heaved my suitcase onto it, and I sat down on the bed in the guest bedroom of his house, where a vase of gerbera daisies in vibrant colors greeted me. In my real life, in my college life in Madison, Wisconsin, I worked at a flower shop, where I sold gerberas and lilies and bunches of alstroemeria. Beside the vase of daisies hung one of my father's paintings, a dedication to me penciled in the corner near his signature. A twin bed stood next to French doors, which opened to an enclosed courtyard, and one wall of the room was painted dandelion yellow, which gave the gerberas a golden hue.

"I love gerbera daisies," I said.

My father looked up from the floor of the closet, where he was rearranging boxes and shoes. "What?"

"The flowers." I gestured toward the vase. "They're my favorite."

He stood up and smiled. "Me, too."

■ ■ ■

I was an adult. I could order a drink at a bar, I lived in an apartment, I did my own grocery shopping and cooking. But now, in Colombia, I was a child again.

On my first morning in my father's house, I came out from my bedroom to see a baby carrier leaning against the wall in the hallway. It was the color of the buttercups that I remembered from my great-grandmother's lake cottage in Minnesota. Made of nylon and aluminum tubing, it looked sturdy but ancient. My father, dressed in track pants and a T-shirt, came from the dining room with a cup of coffee cradled in his hands. He handed it to me and said, "This was yours."

For a split second I thought he was referring to the coffee in my hand. Then I understood he meant the carrier. I had seen photographs of both him and my mother carrying me on their backs in the same kind of contraption. But those photos were in black and white, and I had never known it was yellow. And it was as if my past—the world— was getting colored in like a child's drawing, one object at a time.

"I kept it," he said, kneeling down next to it. And I was afraid, for a moment, that he would want me to climb inside, to re-create a past that he remembered and I didn't. "But now we are giving it to our friends Marcela and Denis who are having a baby."

I leaned against the wall and took a sip of the bitter coffee. For twenty years my father had kept the baby carrier, carting it around from house to house, packing it up with each move, never using it for its intended purpose. Now that I was here in person, perhaps the need for him to keep this memento no longer existed. But it also gave me the feeling that my appearance in his house was somehow a bookend to a story, not the beginning I thought it was.

My father picked up the carrier, hoisted it on one shoulder. And as he held it out like an offering, I noticed his hands. There were traces of green paint under the fingernails. The skin on the backs was dark, age-spotted. These were the hands that changed my diapers, fed me bottles of warm milk, spooned me creamy rice cereal. The hands that never taught me to ride a bike or tie my shoe. The hands that never repaired scraped knees with Band-Aids and kisses. The hands that never loaned me the car keys or pinned a corsage on a strapless dress.

Instead of reaching for the baby carrier or touching his hand, I wrapped mine around the coffee mug again and fled back into my bedroom, shutting the door. He didn't follow me.

During the afternoon of my first day in his house, I sat on the sheltered patio in the backyard, shaded by a lattice of woodwork and vines. My father sipped at his bottle of Club Colombia. I looked at the red-brick expanse that stretched from one bougainvillea to the other, drinking from my own thick bottle of Coke. The smell of citrus circled around me, and I saw two fruit-laden trees—an orange and a lemon.

The abundance of food growing in Colombia was as startling as servants. On the drive from Cali to Popayán, I had seen lush coffee plantations, fields of corn, mango trees in the parks. Here were lemon trees in the backyard, yet I knew people in this country were battling over land and drug money, and children in the streets were begging. But in my father's house in December, when we wanted an orange or a lemon, the only danger, the only difficulty we encountered was the sting of bees or the bite of flies. When all was calm, we just reached through the leaves, and the scent of lemon exploded into the yard as the fruit came off in our hands.

My father smiled benignly as he sipped his beer, as if he saw nothing notable about my first moments in his house, as if we sat on his patio every day surrounded by the bees and the oranges. He no longer noticed the glass shards that protected him from the outside world, and I wondered if there were similar barricades still between us. We looked at one another, not even sure which language to speak in.

"Bueno...," I began.

"So, my dear," said my father.

"Yes?" I answered.

"¿Sí, mi amor?" said my father.

We were trains on opposing tracks, not sure which rail to take.

I can't imagine how my parents were ever able to communicate. My mother spoke nearly flawless Spanish from her years in Colombia, and my father had learned English while a high school student in the

United States, so language wasn't a difficulty. But my father is both overly emotional and fiercely closed off, and my mother reacts to everyone's mood, switching back and forth between bliss and despair. I know they fought, fought about family and nighttime activities and disparate countries. But did they hold hands afterward, did they kiss and make up like couples throughout time? Or did they go their separate ways, close into themselves, seek refuge in silence?

"This is my studio," my father said in English, pointing toward the window behind me.

We left our drinks and entered the room just off the patio. A desk faced the window, and a drafting table stood against a brilliantly painted wall. The wall was the color of dried apricots and stretched at least fifteen feet high. The ceiling and other walls of the studio were barren white and covered with framed posters of my father's designs, paintings on tightly stretched canvases, plaques that honored his work as an artist, a graphic designer, a photographer, and a teacher. On the wall in his studio there were no family photographs but on his desk, under a large piece of glass, he had tucked old pictures. There was one of me as a naked baby, an old school picture of mine, another of an unnamed child, one of a group of strangers smiling and squinting at the camera.

I had seen pictures similar to these in my mother's old photo albums. One features my mother as a young woman with a group of other young, long-haired hippies. I knew it was 1974 because I could see the bulge that was me under her peasant top. My father, with his black hair and black mustache, has his arm slung around her shoulders. As a child I studied this photograph not because I wanted to know what my dad was like but to see if I could unlock the mystery of my own mother, the woman I knew so well and who had this mysterious and alluring history. But when I looked at the slightly blurry outline of her face, she just looked like a pretty young woman, no one in particular, no one of any relation to me. That's how family is. We could be anybody's daughter, father, mother. I was in this foreign country, thousands of miles from all that was familiar, trusting that this man was my blood relation. Sure, there was that roundness of the eyes, the faint shape of the nose, the coloring that didn't come from my mother. But this man was no more familiar to me than the pictures under the glass.

I stood in my father's studio, looking at his desk and his walls and thinking about my mother and why she couldn't stay with her husband, why she left Colombia, why she took me away. In that moment I understood, although I couldn't quite articulate the reasons yet. I knew it had something to do with art and expectations, abandonment and claustrophobia, home and family. And I knew with heartbreaking certainty that part of what I would learn on this trip was the reality of my family's past, the complicated truth of these two people who brought me into the world, the events that had aligned to create the life I was living.

2

I WAS BORN IN COLOMBIA. This is true. I was born in a Spanish-style whitewashed hospital that was later leveled by an earthquake and rebuilt in its likeness. I was born in a small city in the southwestern Colombian mountains, and my father congratulated himself with *tragos* while my mother swore and labored, screamed and pushed.

I began my life in Spanish. This is true. *Zapato* and *leche* were my first words. I crawled on wooden floorboards and encountered tropical insects as big as soup bowls. I teethed on mango seeds, masticating the sweet yellow flesh until my tiny pearls appeared in pink gums. This is true.

And if my mother had never taken me back to the United States, if my parents had never parted, never fought over me, never fell out of love, if I had grown up in that rented house in Colombia, I would have heard the peals of the iron bells of the *iglesia*. When my *amigas* went to mass with their *abuelas,* my hippie parents (a *mezcla* of American progressive values and Colombian pride) would have kept me at home, my mother reading aloud chapters from a dog-eared copy of *Winnie-the-Pooh.*

If we had lived not in a Minneapolis suburb but in a town in South America, I would have watched my mother at her wooden loom, slapping the treadle against the warp with a comforting thud and singing the folksongs of Joni Mitchell. She would have played me scratchy records of Peter, Paul and Mary, and we would have sung along in two-part harmony. These recordings I remember so well from my childhood would have been, had we stayed in Colombia, the only time I would have heard English spoken by anyone other than my parents.

My *abuelitos* would have adored me just as my maternal grand-parents did. I would have been, for a time, the only granddaughter, a perfect excuse for spoiling and indulging. *Dulcitas* and *caramelos* and rides on the shoulders of my *abuelo* would have been mine.

I would have worn my mother's hand-sewn clothes embroidered with her original abstract flowers and designs. When my mother taught English, I would have stayed with a *primo* or the *vecino* next door. The neighbors would have fed me *café con leche* and taught me to dance the *cumbia,* wanting to mold me into a true *Colombiana.*

The house was at one end of a single-lane bridge where cars and *camionetas* waited for their turn to cross, and with my father's radical-ized ideals and my mother's midwestern upbringing, we would have lived in a sort of comfortable isolation in our traditional town. I would have been a happy child, pampered and loved.

My parents would not have been happy. The nights my father spent locked in his *taller* painting away the hours would have made my mother silent in loneliness, wishing for her Minnesota parents, her brothers, her American girlfriends. She and I would have tiptoed around the drafty *casa,* where she scrubbed clothes by hand over a large, rough stone, until my father emerged, splattered in paint, ex-hausted and self-congratulatory.

My mother would have flown into an occasional rage that would have been borne of legitimate frustrations. My father and I would have sought refuge in flowers and walks on sun-dappled trails. He would have set up a miniature easel next to his own, and we would have painted pastoral scenes side by side until my mother's soprano rendition of "Blowin' in the Wind" came floating up into the hills above our house. My father and I would have marched home through the high-altitude jungle to kiss and make up, the picture of familial bliss for another couple of days.

If I would have been living in Popayán when I was eight, I would have been there when an earthquake hit our town, and I would have been with my cousins buying bread in the *panadería.* There would have been a tremble and great rush as if the ocean were suddenly overtaking the coastal mountains. The moment when my *primo* Renzito was struck by falling fragments from the ovens would have been repeated over and over in my childhood nightmares. The brick missed his head—*gracias a Dios*—but the scar on his shoulder would have always been a reminder of the earth moving. My auntie would have rushed us out into the dust-filled plaza, and, when it was over, the equatorial sun would have laughed at the debris nature had left us.

Even though my family would have been the only non-Catholics, we would have gone to gawk at the Pope when he came to bless our devastated town. I would have remembered very little of the visit from *el Papa,* only the crowds and the vendors selling hand-painted plaques in the shape of his hat. My father wouldn't have bought me one, and since I would have been unaccustomed to being told no, my hot, selfish tears would have made the people around us assume we had lost loved ones in the *terremoto.* My mother would have found this to be another reason she should never have left the United States.

By fifteen, I would have come back from a visit to the United States to find that my best friend's *hermano* had been killed by guerrillas. The brother would have been just seventeen. He would have saved up for a *motocicleta* and would have taken off on a rosy October morning to drive into the *páramo.* He and his *amigos* would have been young, beautiful boys with short, black buzz cuts and would have started *la universidad* the next year. I would have been half in love with one of the *hermano*'s friends, although I never would have admitted it. And when all seven boys, mistaken for military, were shot in the knees before being shot dead in the back, I would have imagined them, as I do now, face down on a winding mountain road, the shiny coffee leaves and giant sugar cane shading the bikes, which lay abandoned on the gravel, a vicious *guerrilla* killing that would have made no sense to me or to the families in the *pueblo.*

When I went to a big midwestern university—assuming I even went to college—my accent would have been stilted and cautious. Even though my mother would have spoken English to me had we stayed in Colombia, there would have been holes in my vocabulary, experiences that set me apart. I wouldn't have had a *quinceñera,* but I wouldn't have gone to prom either. I would have earned As in English class at *la colegia,* but I would have strained to understand the subtitled episodes of *Saved by the Bell,* which I would have watched not on a looming color TV in the basement of the house on Edgerton but on a small black-and-white *tele* at the foot of my parents' bed.

At home in Colombia, I would always have been viewed as the outsider. My skin would have been lighter than the other *muchachos* in our neighborhood. My German legs and ankles, clearly descended from my mother's Anglo Saxon roots, would have made me self-conscious in front of my Colombian *amigas*—girls with the slender bodies of *indios.*

And whenever I visited my mother's family in the United States, I would have found myself even more of an outsider. I would have been pasted with labels: Hispanic, foreigner, Latina, minority. My English would have been grammatically exact but colloquially forced, and my Spanish wouldn't have been like the more familiar drawn-out rhythm of *mexicanos.*

If I somehow had still met my future husband, and if I had brought this *gringo* back to Colombia to meet my parents, my father would have given him a Colombian kiss on the cheek and then called him "dude" to show he was cool. My mother would have been standoffish but secretly relieved that I was marrying an American.

But my newlywed life in the United States would have found me as confused as my mismatched parents. I would have pined for the humidity of the valleys and the crisp air of *las montañas.* I would have spent my money on long-distance phone calls to friends in Bogotá, Quito, Cartagena. I would have found myself simultaneously homesick and at home. I would have discovered that my handsome *esposo* didn't always understand my accented English, didn't like the *sancocho* or deathly sweet *café con panela* I prepared for him. We would have had to compromise when the days became endless and *las noches* filled with arguments, fighting, misunderstandings—all those problems that arise from a joining and a clash of two cultures. And like my mother before me, I would have had to decide which life I wanted.

But this, all this, it isn't what happened: this isn't the life my mother chose, this isn't the life I lived.

I was born in Colombia. This is true.

3

MY MOTHER NEVER TOLD ME *not* to contact my father, but she had also never encouraged me. When his letters arrived at my grandparents' house (she never gave him our current address), she would hand them over without a word. It wasn't until I was fifteen and living with my stepfamily that I wrote "Dear Dad" for the first time, and any armchair psychologist will see the impetus for an only child to contact her father at that point, however distant and estranged he might be. I don't remember now how I figured out how many stamps to affix to the envelope, and I don't know whether I visited a post office or simply lifted the red flag at home, but I do remember enclosing a school picture (me with hair-sprayed bangs and cheekbones just beginning to emerge from behind slowly receding baby fat) and licking the sticky seam of the envelope. I didn't know until much later how my first letter to my father impacted his—and ultimately my—life. The notebook paper, the slanted words written in ballpoint pen, the photograph with its unevenly cut borders: these things became immediate keepsakes for him, artifacts of change.

After sending the letter, I unlatched the black metal mailbox at the end of the driveway every day after school before anyone else got home, hoping to intercept any return communication from him. Now I wonder if the furtive letter writing was a symptom of a genetic propensity for silence. When a letter did arrive, I kept it secret, clinging to the ownership of a real father, even if it was one I didn't know. Like many moments in life, this one marked an invisible line that would divide then from now, what happened from what didn't.

This line appeared again when, at age twenty-one, I heard his voice for the first time.

"Hello, my dear Anika," he had said. It was during a birthday party in my ugly student apartment in Madison, my friends and Dave, whom I would marry years later, drinking beer and making noise in the background.

"Happy birthday," said the voice like someone chewing on willow sticks.

It wasn't, I recognized later, the first time I had heard his voice, but it was the first time I could remember.

"My wife and I want to send you a ticket to come to Colombia."

When I used to ask my mother about their divorce, she told me it was because she wanted to live in Minnesota and he loved Colombia too much to leave it. This oversimplification had satisfied my curiosity as a child, but suddenly, standing amid clinking beer bottles and collapsing birthday cake, I needed to know what kind of power this country had that would make a man choose a place over a person. I needed to know if returning to my birthplace would give me a grounding in life, if getting to know my father would make me feel like other people—if somehow that country could help me fit in with my life, my relationships, my future, the world.

"Yes," I had told him recklessly. "Yes, I want to come to Colombia."

Each action has an equal and opposite reaction, so here I was three months after that phone call, sightseeing in Colombia. That first week my father brought me to the old part of Popayán, known as *la ciudad blanca,* the "white city," because its colonial Spanish architecture and character have been preserved since its conquistador founding in 1537. The center of town is all whitewashed buildings with red tile roofs. Many of the buildings were destroyed by the earthquake in 1983, but afterward each ruined structure was rebuilt in exact imitation of the centuries-old style. The city has a park, Pueblito Patojo, that pays tribute to its architecture, a miniature town with replicas of the important buildings with roofs about one-third normal height, making me feel oversized and clumsy.

I crossed Parque Caldas, the large main plaza, as I returned from mailing postcards at the post office. The plaza was ringed by trees and flowering bushes. Vendors pushed carts with bags of sweets and bottles of soda. Shoe shiners set up shop in the shade. I passed by the elderly couples and mothers with perambulators that rested on the benches surrounding the statue of Francisco José de Caldas, one of the fathers of Colombia's independence. My own father sat on one of the benches, a cigarette in one hand, knees splayed, relaxed. He always wore a vest—a photographer's vest with plenty of room for rolls of film and extra lenses, although usually all he kept in the pockets were a couple of cigarettes and a few pesos.

When I was near enough to hear him, he said, "I thought I saw a ghost."

I sat down beside him on the bench.

"You looked just like Nance," he said, referring to my mother, Nancy, by her family nickname. "The way you walk. I remember her walking across the plaza just like that."

I smiled like I always do.

"I thought you were a ghost."

My mother and I look alike, can always be identified as mother and daughter. We have the same wide smiles, the same gummy teeth. We have had similar body shapes our entire lives but with our own highlights. My stomach was always flatter than hers; her knees were always nicer than mine. (She always told me I had my *tía* Josefina's knees; this was not a compliment.)

When I was young and there were just the two of us, I used to lounge on her bed and help her pick out clothes. I remember going through my mother's jewelry and deciding what went with that sweater, with that blouse, with those shoes. I remember exactly what my mother looked like when I was ten and she was thirty-five. I remember her fleshy belly and her slightly dimpled thighs. I remember her smooth white back and her loose underwear.

But in 1970, when she was nineteen years old, she was thin with wispy light brown hair, almost blonde. She favored an oversized Boy

Scout shirt, army green. She met Melinda, who would become a sort of aunt to me, just before leaving for Colombia, the two of them the only students from their college who chose Colombia for their semester abroad.

Colombia. Populated by Spanish descendants, African slaves, European refugees, and indigenous people. Ravaged by alternating periods of war and democracy. By the end of 1969, when Nancy and Melinda booked their tickets, *La Violencia* of the 1940s to 1960s had calmed, but the guerrilla group, the FARC, was increasing in power and ruthlessness. This political reality did not affect these two girls' plans. They went to Colombia.

Nancy and Melinda lived in a boardinghouse in Cali and became friends through proximity. They arrived just after Christmas during *las Navidades,* the weeks-long celebration born of the country's Catholic roots, and the women learned slang, tried new foods, drank local beer. They shopped for hand-knitted sweaters and emerald jewelry.

In the boardinghouse, my mother and Melinda met Ginny. She already spoke fluent, angular Spanish and introduced them to the life of American girls in Colombia, to others like Beth and Barbara and Dan. There were the local college boys. There were *fiestas* and impromptu outings with Peace Corps volunteers and wanderers and hippies. There were the daily walks to the Centro Colombo Americano to teach English, the meals with the other boarders.

Colombian men in the streets would heckle the three girls until Ginny talked back and gestured rudely. My mother watched Ginny's daring with admiration, and I picture my mother, tugging at her miniskirt as she passed these bold, dark men. Her pale cheeks redden easily. She has always been too quick to smile, a reflex from her childhood.

And it wasn't long before she found a boyfriend. Seth—was he the first one? He was blond and tall. Or was he brown-haired and heavy? All that really mattered was that Seth introduced Nancy to his former roommate, a bearded *Colombiano* a few years older than the college students. An artist, a man with an easy laugh, a way with women, a charming and disarming personality.

I picture my mother walking the streets of Cali with Renzo, the Colombian artist. He is just her height, barely five foot six. In all the old photographs she is wearing a ruana, a sheep's wool poncho, and smiling broadly. The whitewashed buildings of Popayán charmed her, its cobbled streets enchanted her. In June that year, Melinda boarded a plane and returned to a changed United States; the Beatles had fallen apart, blood had been shed at Kent State, and the war in Vietnam was under scrutiny. My mother stayed in Colombia, making her own changes, her own choices. She enrolled in school in Popayán. She moved in with Renzo, set up house. When he fell ill and was hospitalized, she hurried through white corridors and past nuns in habits and waited by his bedside. His mother referred to Nancy as *la nuera,* the daughter-in-law. Even though she wasn't, not really, not yet.

"I thought you were your mother for a moment," my father said and smoked his cigarette, and we stared into the distance or the past. I could imagine my mother. I could imagine her, my age, walking across the plaza. But I didn't see any ghosts. I saw strangers, the people of Popayán busy in their days. My father looked across the plaza and saw my mother. Perhaps my father's eyes misted as he saw ghosts, as he saw me as my mother, me as my infant self.

But I wanted to tell my father, *I am not a ghost.* I do not look like my mother. I do not look like my grandmother. I am unique. I am different. *See this dark hair?* I wanted to say. *See these brown eyes?* These are yours. I am not a ghost. I am a new person, a flesh and blood person totally and completely made by you and my mother. I am here now. My mother is not here. I am not her. I am not a ghost.

I said nothing, and the smoke from his cigarette drifted across the cobbles.

4

MY BEDROOM IN MY FATHER'S HOUSE is saturated in him. The yellow wall, the daisies, the paintings he has framed for me. A Guambiano Indian. An African woman hauling bundles on her head. Clay roof tiles and whitewashed buildings. With tint and charcoal, he has managed to capture Colombia in this room. And even though I have been here only a few days, I feel captured.

I pull back the curtains on the French doors in my room, desperate for a breath of fresh air. The courtyard between my bedroom window and the dining room is bright with cloud-filtered light. It is both inside and outside. It is sheltered and also exposed. Crickets hop into my room. Who doesn't belong here?

I think of my former stepfamily's house back in Minnesota and how out of place I had felt there. And then, just as I became resigned to that life, my mother decisively ended that marriage, too. I remember how confident she had seemed, how certain, although now I understand that, of course, she had done this before—this leaving a marriage. My mother told me that in those final months during my last year in high school she had been secretly collecting her most precious belongings and moving them, piece by piece, to a self-storage locker. Her grandmother's china, old photo albums, the breadmaker. How, I had wondered, did she choose the things she wanted to save?

The evening after she told me we were leaving, my stepfather held our last family meeting from the confines of his La-Z-Boy recliner, which opened its menacing jaws. "Nancy and I are getting divorced," he said, and I could see that his two sons were hearing the news for the first time. But I couldn't really think about them anymore. I was glad I was the only child, the only one.

I was so embarrassed to have those two stepbrothers. They were unruly puppies, had never been properly housebroken. When I first became part of this jumbled family, the stepbrothers were at home only every other week. I was left on my own during those quiet times, while my mother and her husband did their newlywed thing. I hibernated in the reclusion of a big stephouse, scanning *Seventeen* magazines, watching the new phenomenon of music videos on a TV bigger than any I had ever seen before. Then the stepbrothers would begin their week at the house, and chaos would whirl around me. How could it not have? I wonder now. They were two boys whose lives were demarcated by Sundays, by the switch between houses, neither of which was really home. They had outbursts of tears and shouting as if they couldn't control their own actions—and no one else could control them either. This was before diagnoses of attention deficit disorder and before Ritalin was prescribed for children with no impulse control. This was before social workers connected the dots between fathers with abusive pasts and their troubled sons. But even if I had understood the complexities of their psyches and lives then, it still wouldn't have prevented my resentment, my aversion. They were not just a couple of hyperactive boys; they represented all that was my new life. When they were around, I counted down the hours until they would leave again.

I hated living with my stepfamily, hated my stepfather. It hadn't been my idea, and I have never liked things that weren't my idea. Being part of that family was like role-playing for me. I never fully engaged, was always waiting for the curtain call. In the five years I lived with this assortment of people called my blended family, I had never bonded, never cared for them, never even respected them. Did I? I loved my mother fiercely, but I hated the way her marriage had changed everything in my life, hated the way the marriage had changed her. I had been an only child for the first thirteen years of my life, and sharing wasn't a skill I had ever mastered. I always imagined myself a little like Cinderella—only with stepbrothers and a stepfather. I was the oldest, the girl, the one who had to mow the lawn, skim the pool, cook, vacuum. We were wealthy now that we were living on my stepfather's salary, but I would have preferred our food-shelf salad dressing to the grilled steaks. I was resentful of his demands and expectations. My mother was too downtrodden to stick up for me, too caught up in the drama of pleasing an unpleasant man to have energy left over for a self-reliant teenager. There were the forced hoedown nights when everyone gathered around my stepfather and his banjo. His sons sang uproariously, and I was embarrassed for all of us. I strummed the autoharp and wished I was somewhere else, wished my mother wouldn't play along, wouldn't pick at her guitar with such willingness. Everyone pretended they were happy to strum old, out-of-tune instruments and wonder what to do with a drunken sailor. But, in truth, no one cared. At one point my mother and her husband talked briefly of having another child. She was only in her late thirties and, as a romantic teenager, I thought that a baby could repair this family. But they knew they needed to fix whatever was wrong before having more children. I should have known that a baby doesn't solve a marriage's problems; it hadn't solved my parents'.

Once, in an attempt to forge a relationship with me, a temperamental teen, my stepfather took me out on his brand-new BMW motorcycle. The bike was his latest shiny and expensive new toy (this was before my mother gave herself third-degree burns when leaning too close to the exhaust pipe). I remember how I tried to balance without wrapping my arms around his waist. My head rattled around in the yellow helmet and seemed to shut off my brain. My body was there, exposed, experiencing this ride, but my mind was disconnected.

When my mother and I moved our things out of the house and into a second-floor walk-up apartment, the first snow of winter began to fall. The brown grass and leafless trees were methodically dusted in white, erasing their sharp lines and hard edges as if the past itself was being wiped out. How easily the past could disappear if you let it.

■ ■ ■

In my father's house, I watch a tiny bird the same color as the baby carrier fly into the courtyard between my room and the dining room. The broken bottles that top the walls are no obstacle for her turmeric wings. After soaking in the nectar of a bright-pink hibiscus, she takes a wrong turn. Instead of darting upward and out of the courtyard, she swoops through the dining room and then lands on the glass coffee table in the living room. She taps at her reflection and chirps several times before finally making her escape.

I let the sheer curtain fall, obscuring my view of the bird as she flies out of the airy and open house. In my stocking feet, I run silently through the tiled hallway and out into the yard behind the house. My breath catches in a jagged gasp before I exhale.

5

WHEN SHE CAME TO THE REALIZATION that she was trapped, she was twenty-five and had an infant under the age of one. She was trapped in a drafty house, couldn't leave, couldn't pack up the moment she felt ensnared, couldn't escape in the middle of the night like a cat burglar. She had a baby.

I've seen the house. It's at the end of a country road near a single-lane bridge. The house as I saw it was big and airy, ceramic tiles worn from decades of footsteps, a slightly overgrown courtyard out back with a dry fountain. Renzo and Nancy rented the house—half the house—from the widow who owned it. She had divided the house in two with thin wallboard, right down the center of the living room. They lived in the half of the house where the woman's husband had shot himself. Worn with debt and despair, the man had chosen the living room for his last breaths. And my young parents lived in that house with their infant—me. This is where my mother was trapped.

The house had no phone, was miles from town, and they had no car. Nancy washed diapers by hand, let them dry in the noon sun. Renzo worked at the university and then stayed downtown after work to drink, to paint, to . . . ? I imagine her, with a twinge of the same postpartum depression I later experienced, sitting in the haunted living room, crickets jumping through the open doors, a baby playing at her feet. She is waiting. Alone, with only an unhappy ghost for company.

The neighbor across the street befriended her, a woman whose husband was also a professor. There was another *vecina* down the street, another sometime companion. No replacement for a constant husband, though. Through the thin walls of the house, the widow must have heard the shouting, the arguments.

Don Julio would arrive unannounced to visit his only grand-daughter.

"Ay, mi niñacita," Don Julio would cry as he tossed his baby grand-daughter into the air like a ripe mango. "Te quiero, I love you."

Nancy couldn't fault her father-in-law for his love for the baby, but she felt invaded and exposed. Doña Rosa and Don Julio were in the midst of escaping their own troubles. Financial difficulties, the collapse of Doña Rosa's family hotel, the end of a car dealership. Un-able to support themselves, they moved in with their son Harold and his wife, Elvia, and young son, Renzito.

Renzo and Nancy, too, had difficulty supporting themselves. There was never enough cash, there were hours of loneliness. And there were the rumors and *chismes* about affairs and disloyalty. Nancy heard about the women and knew about the late nights.

She taught English in town, contributed something to the house-hold expenses, left the house a couple times a week. Don Julio arranged for a friend, a taxi driver, to take her into town. She was uncomfortable teaching, though; she didn't like standing in front of a class. One day a woman in her class collapsed. A young woman. Maybe a blood clot from first-generation birth control pills. Nancy knew CPR and rushed to her, administered mouth-to-mouth resuscitation. The young woman died, one of Nancy's many guilty regrets from that time. But she became a hero for the attempt at lifesaving. Her life was becoming intricately woven into the fabric of the town. She was being tied down with wool and cotton, strung up into unrecognizable patterns.

Please send me a book on divorce, Nancy wrote to her parents. On the lonely nights when her husband was in the cafés, she studied the book and learned the minutiae of ending a marriage, the steps you must take to undo the vows and promises. Divorce didn't become legal in the heavily Catholic country until 1991, but that didn't stop marriages from falling apart. Along with antiquated rules on dissolving marriages, Colombia's custody laws were equally patriarchal. As if the country had foreseen the difficulties of multicultural marriage and procreation, fathers were granted custodial rights to their children. Without a father's permission, offspring cannot exit the country.

"I'm going to Minnesota," Nancy told her husband. She told him she would take the baby for a visit, planning all along to never return.

"Let's go," Renzo said. And suddenly it was a family vacation.

How do you escape a bad marriage and a foreign country? If you had wings you would fly over the walls, scale the mountains, carry your child on your back. If you were a young woman, a woman desperate and confused and angry, you would use trickery and cunning.

Renzo and Nancy and the baby arrived in Minnesota in August 1976. From the stoop of their midcentury rambler, her parents welcomed them with open arms, smiles of complicity pasted on their faces.

Nancy had retained a lawyer—not a very good one, but she would do. Nancy waited for the right moment, a time when the baby was not with them. She didn't want to compete with a toddling baby while she told her husband she wanted a divorce.

Renzo wanted to work things out, did not grasp the enormity of the chasm between them. He wanted to try counseling, he wanted to repair the union. She did not. She didn't love him anymore, and she was deaf to his arguments. She had made up her mind. He was not the love of her life.

The trouble with an international divorce is the child. Who will care for this child? What culture, which country will this child live in? What language will this child speak?

"Anika is coming back with me," Renzo told his wife. He bought two plane tickets to return to Colombia.

And so the mother whisked the baby away. She took her away from her father. She took the baby to an undisclosed location; not even her parents could know where they were. First it was the family's land in northern Minnesota, where the mother and child sought refuge in a log cabin with no running water. Not knowing where his daughter was, Renzo went to the Colombian consulate. Because this is what you will do to keep your child.

Renzo and the consul drove slowly through the suburban neighborhood of his wife's childhood, watching for a young woman, searching for a child.

"Where are they?" the consul questioned the maternal grandparents.

"We don't know," they answered honestly. This had been part of the plan. The intricate plan. Because this is what you will do to keep your child.

Renzo returned to Colombia alone. Nancy kept the baby. They both escaped, and everybody lost something.

6

A SMALL, BROWN-HAIRED GIRL sits at the second desk from the right. It is 1981. The girl is near enough to the bank of windows to watch the evergreens fill up with snow. To her left is a blond boy named Chris—one of four in the first grade—and behind her is a skinny girl named Deborah. Beyond Deborah, she spots Mandy's yellow pigtails curling beneath red bows of thick yarn.

They are all bent over their papers, the room quiet. Ms. Brinkman walks back and forth between the desks. They are the kind of desks that open on top, leaving room inside for workbooks and pencil boxes. This little girl's pencil box has an incomplete set of colored pencils—the pink went missing, and she thinks Valerie took it. There is also a tiny bottle of Elmer's Glue with its irresistible coating of clear, dried glue on its orange tip. She likes to reach into the pencil box and pick at the glue, hoping it will come off in one piece, making a tiny cone.

Every desk has an identical worksheet on it and five crayons. Each child has chosen crayons from Ms. Brinkman's gallon bucket. The title on the paper says: "My family eats breakfast." There is a large square with a cartoonish table. The assignment is to draw your family at the table and fill the table with the food you eat for breakfast.

The little brown-haired girl is confident. She's a good student, learning to read and write. She understands the task perfectly and prides herself on her artistic skills. She knows that she is naturally artistic because her father—a man she knows is her father but doesn't know at all—is an artist, who occasionally sends her sketches through international mail. She has spent many, many hours with blank paper. She used to have a packet of markers until her mother learned of the possible dangers the ink could inflict on a growing child. Then the markers were replaced with colored pencils and crayons, tools never as satisfying as felt-tipped markers. She is sometimes allowed to use her mother's sketch pad, one that is filled with charcoal renderings of flowers, shells, hands, and even a nude. She skips past the sketch of the naked man to find fresh, clean paper. The little girl has a rough understanding of perspective, is learning that objects meant to seem farther away will be smaller.

The little brown-haired girl carefully draws her family: first there is a figure with short hair, glasses, and an apron. This figure has a broad smile on her face, and the hands have been drawn clutching a coffee cup with two squiggly lines of steam rising up. The second figure is markedly smaller than the first, a miniature version of the other one, this time with long hair. The little girl chooses a darker-brown crayon to make the child's hair, but she uses the same red to make another smile. The table is piled high with pancakes, a bottle that surely must be syrup, and a square of yellow butter. A lopsided pitcher holds something orange and liquidy, two cups filled with the same color.

"You need to draw your whole family," Ms. Brinkman says as she leans over the little girl's desk, the scent of stale coffee and face powder drifting down.

The little girl looks at the paper her teacher is holding. She sees her family, expertly drawn, at the table.

"I did."

"No, honey, your whole family. Where's your daddy?"

The little girl looks down at the paper and then back up at her teacher. Ms. Brinkman is pretty and round, a sort of human version of Miss Piggy. She wears beautifully tailored clothing, favoring pink and pale yellow. Her eyes and lips are accentuated with thick makeup, and her skin is a darker shade than you might expect to find on a blonde in January in Minnesota.

"I don't have a dad."

"Of course you do," says the teacher. "Families have a mom and a dad."

The little girl brings the paper home to her mother.

"I was supposed to draw my whole family."

"Very nice. What are they eating?" her mother asks her.

She smiles. "Pancakes."

"Is that what we eat for breakfast?"

"Sometimes," the little girl admits. Usually they don't eat pancakes. More often there might be oatmeal, Cream of Wheat, or thick whole-wheat toast with jam.

"Ms. Brinkman said I was supposed to draw my dad."

Her mother is silent.

The next day her mother picks her up from school. She walks down the hallway, grasping her daughter's hand. Her mother never comes to school except for conferences. Teachers never have anything negative to say about this little girl. Her mother is like her; she is a rule follower, a smiler and a nodder.

"Ms. Brinkman? Do you have a minute?"

The teacher's magenta-painted lips part into a gleaming smile. She is good at being a teacher, good at talking to both parents and children. She is musical, has a piano in her first-grade classroom. She could have been in the opera, but she damaged her vocal chords. Even still there is something operatic about her, and she still knows how to own a room.

"Come in, Mrs. Fajardo."

The little girl's mother is not a "Mrs." She is not married. She is an anomaly in this 1980s suburban city.

The little girl chooses crayons from Ms. Brinkman's bucket while her mother and her teacher talk.

"Don't tell my daughter what a family is," she hears her mother say. She pulls out the portrait. "This is our family," she says, pointing to the drawing.

Mother and daughter.

7

WE STROLLED THROUGH THE STREETS of Popayán after a leisurely lunch at a restaurant in the center of town. It was late afternoon, and the downtown was quiet, restful. The sun beat down on the dusty streets, and my father pointed out landmarks and architectural interests.

"Wow," I said.

"How interesting," I said.

And then I said, "I'm going to be sick."

There is that one instant of absolute certainty when you know you're about to be sick. It's so quick you don't usually have time to think about where you will be sick, why you are sick, whether you want to be sick.

He rushed me into a little café and called out: "¿El baño? ¿Dónde está el baño?"

Without so much as a glance our way, the proprietress waved in the direction of the little restroom, but it was too late. I lost my entire lunch right there on the tile floor of this little café. I was too sick to really know or care what was going on around me, but I remember my father taking a mop from someone and wiping my vomit from the floor. Part of me knew I should be embarrassed having this man—essentially a stranger—clean up after me. But I also had a moment of clarity when I remembered how often my mother had had her chance to swab my damp brow, mop bodily fluids.

I had been a bed wetter as a young child. My mother would awaken to my cries and come into my room, hauling me out of bed by one arm. I stood as still as stone at the other end of the room as my mother stripped the wet sheets and found fresh ones, the light from the hall streaming into the room. The wet cotton underwear stuck to my legs as she pulled it off. She wanted me to go to the bathroom, but by that time my bladder was empty.

I had a physical excuse for the bed-wetting. My early childhood was filled with toileting and elimination issues. After suffering from one infection after another, the doctors in Minnesota discovered their cause. When I was barely three years old, I had to have bladder surgery to correct a birth defect. Congenital ureter abnormality. It had something to do with tubes and valves. Surgery solved the problem and even saved my life. My mother has told me that the surgery was one reason she can never regret leaving Colombia, bringing me to the United States. In her mind, she inflated the dangers that could have claimed my life, and this tiny, invisible birth defect was one of them. I don't know if a hospital in South America would have given me any different care or if this is just a balm she rubs on her regret. But I can imagine now what it must have been like to watch a feverish child whose body is trying to fight the constant bladder infections, whose body can't seem to perform the most basic of human functions. Had we lived in Colombia in the late 1970s, the chances of my receiving the care I needed would have been slim. In Minnesota, we had access to good medical care, money and insurance to pay for it, and the comfort of sterile hospitals and semiprivate rooms.

I remember being wheeled to surgery, I remember the bright lights over my head and the nurses and doctors talking. This memory would come back with jarring lucidity when I was wheeled into an operating room at the age of thirty-two to have my baby via emergency Caesarean. There is a feeling of absolute loss of control when you are transported on your back on a gurney. You can't see where you're going or where you've been. The present—with its overhead lights coming in and out of view—is all that you have for reference. You lose track of who and where you are, and you give up, give in, surrender.

After the successful bladder surgery, I spent several days in the hospital. I shared my room with a little girl, who cried when it was time for her to go home. I watched with disbelief as she fought getting her shoes on. Her father cajoled, and the nurses smiled. I remember watching and wishing I were in her place, wishing I was the one going home, wishing to be anywhere but in that dark hospital room.

My mother stayed with me every night, tried to sleep sitting upright in hard hospital chairs listening to the hums and beeps of the unit. One night she took a respite and went back to her bed for a much-needed night of sleep and a shower. It was that night, though, that I remember. I awoke in the semidarkness of the hospital room and screamed. A nurse in scratchy white cotton took me to the nurses' station and settled me on her lap. It wasn't a children's hospital, and I'm sure the nurse's job description didn't include comforting hysterical three-year-olds. My mother never left me again during that hospital stay.

After he mopped the café's floor, my father drove me home in the Suzuki, the dirt roads of the neighborhood jolting my poisoned stomach until I cried. He helped me into the house, and I immediately threw up again. When Ceci got home, they tucked me into their big, queen-sized bed. Their room had an en suite bathroom, and the toilet was a few steps away from the bed. I didn't always make it. My father cleaned up after me again while I lay prone, as helpless as a baby.

My father called a doctor—a friend, I'm sure (my father was friends with everyone). The doctor came with an actual black bag and brought me some kind of electrolyte drink. I couldn't keep that down either. For two or three days I vomited.

When I was a baby, my parents used cloth diapers fastened with pastel-colored diaper pins. My mother scrubbed them on a washboard. My father also changed diapers. He cared for me while my mother went to work teaching English. He changed me and burped me. But only for the first two years. That's all he had: two years of *caca*-filled diapers and cuddles, of lullabies and baby food, of chubby bellies and shrieking cries. While he escaped most of the more unpleasant parts of parenthood, he also missed out on the best. The image of him mopping my vomit from the floor of a café gives me some satisfaction. After my bout of food poisoning, I felt kinder toward him, felt like he was more mine, more my father.

8

WE WERE ON OUR WAY TO HIKE at La Laguna de San Rafael in Puracé National Park, and Ceci, who was driving the Suzuki, pulled over on the side of the road somewhere in the hills outside Popayán.

"Mira," Ceci said, leaning forward to point at something out the windshield. "That's the Puracé volcano."

In the distance I could see the fuzzy outline of a mountain. Although I was born in the Andes, I knew almost nothing about mountains. I had grown up with Minnesota's endless prairies and pine forests that engulf you. In a midwestern landscape, there is less to wonder about, more, I think, that is visible and obvious, right in front of you. Minnesota, with the exception of a few fairies I saw when I was eight, is barren of magic. It is a solid place built on bedrock where the ground doesn't move and mountains don't spew volcanic ash.

"Don't worry," Ceci added. "The volcano hasn't erupted since 1977."

In 1977 I had been three years old, far removed from my beginnings in Colombia. By then I was already in Minnesota with my mother. I had already become an American.

When we reached a high plain above the tree line, my father gestured at the rugged landscape. "This is the páramo. It's like a cold rain forest."

I have since learned that he confused his definitions, a páramo being nothing like a rain forest but rather an ecosystem sometimes described as tropical alpine tundra. And yet, he explained it with such authority and clarity, it made me wonder what version of truth he lives.

"In Puracé," he said, "you can see four ecosystems: forest, subpáramo, páramo, and snow. Can you believe it? Snow, just like in Minnesota."

My father had been gleeful in this lecture. Snow fascinated him in a way unknown to people who grow up around the stuff. He loved the study of white on white, the exploration of shadow and color. His art was filled with blank spaces as if everything could be explained by omission. Now I wonder if his art has always been an extension of the way his mind works; secrets are part of the whole, a necessary texture that makes everything around them stand out.

"Those are *frailejones*," Ceci said, pointing again. I could only assume she meant the little treelike plants that dotted the open field of the páramo.

"Monks," my father translated for me. "Don't they look like little men?"

When I looked back at the field, I could see armies bobbing and weaving in the wind, like the attackers that Don Quixote must have battled. It put me on edge, that recognition that we were all perhaps one anthropomorphic succulent away from insanity. And that was when Ceci stopped the car again.

I looked out the window to see what sight she was showing me now. But there was no panorama. Instead I saw a military vehicle in the middle of the road. At least it looked like a military vehicle to me. It was painted a dull color, very dark, maybe black or green. Three men (or maybe just two) stood in front of the truck, feet wide apart, hands on automatic rifles.

Ceci pulled on the emergency brake with a loud creak, and my father reached between the seats to lay a hand on my shoulder. The men stood beside their truck, holding machine guns cradled in their arms like the bouquets of flowers the soprano accepts at the end of an opera. And in a way it almost looked a performance, the men with their guns posing like stereotypes of Colombia's dangers. I had been immunized against hepatitis A and B, typhoid, and tuberculosis and given a bottle of malaria pills (even though Popayán's altitude keeps mosquitoes away). But I was happy to take those remedies because I didn't know how else to prepare for this place, how to be safe. Even though I knew there was no vaccination to protect against violence or bad luck. Or heartache.

We watched one of the men walk toward us. He walked with the self-assurance of someone holding a weapon that can kill you; his movements were sure and solid without any hesitation. I'm not sure how afraid I was then because even as I remember this moment, the reality of my fear chokes me. I needed to be afraid, and the thought that I didn't know enough to be afraid makes me even more frightened for the version of me at twenty-one who watched the barrels of rifles approach.

The man stood at the driver's side. He had clear brown skin and inscrutable eyes. Ceci rested her forearm on the open window. She said nothing.

"Get out," said the man. "Get out, leave the car."

Suddenly everything seemed to happen in fast-forward. Before I knew how it happened, I was climbing out of the Suzuki followed closely by my father, who said under his breath, "Whatever you do, don't open your mouth."

I would have obeyed anyone who told me what to do at that moment, but there was something about being commanded by my father that felt both reassuring and strange. If I had grown up with him, would he have told me to eat my spinach, clean my room, brush my teeth? Perhaps if there had been shared custody, a coming and going of weekends and summer vacations, I would have tried to get away with not listening to him. He might have been the parent I could have manipulated, smiled sweetly at, and kissed on the cheek. I might have become skilled at persuasion and argument, letting my role as daughter give me an edge over doing what I was told. But even if that had happened, I would still have kept my mouth shut that day. There was an urgency in his voice that let me know that this was a matter beyond either of us, beyond decisions and thinking. This was a time to follow, not lead.

The three of us stood down the road a couple dozen feet from the Suzuki as the men searched it. We were just three more bobbing heads, as immobile as the *frailejones*. Ceci and my father were calm but said nothing as we waited. When I had told my mother before my flight that I was afraid, I had not thought beyond the danger of plane crashes. Even my overactive imagination didn't have the vocabulary to conjure barrels of guns and the crunch of boots on gravel. I had been using fear as a placeholder for the anxiety I felt about meeting my father and the fear of finding out about my parents and my family and, ultimately, myself. But here was a different kind of danger, a danger real and palpable. A bird called to its mate as we stood together in the road, and somewhere in the valley below us a truck ground its gears.

At last the soldiers, rifles at their sides, motioned us back to the Suzuki. As the men stepped aside, Ceci put the car into gear again and swerved around their truck. As we left them in the dust of our tires, my father said, "If you would have spoken, they would have known you weren't Colombian."

I didn't ask what he meant by that. I was already learning that if you don't want to know the answers, you shouldn't ask the questions.

9

MY FATHER AND I WALKED ARM IN ARM through the streets of Cali as if we had been walking like this our whole lives. We had just eaten flatbread and tahini at my father's favorite restaurant, and we stopped near the fountain in the middle of a plaza, where baobabs and coconut trees leaned over us. We sat on a bench as if we were not strangers. And in the darkness of this Colombian night, the sound of water drumming in my ears, I could believe it. He pulled a single cigarette from his breast pocket but did not light it. There was a momentary, contemplative stillness as we sat side by side.

"I fell in a fountain once," I told him. The two of us had come to Cali for a couple days of sightseeing in the tropical city, and we needed a story. This one would fill in the space between us. Stories have that kind of power. "I was walking along the edge of this fountain when I was little," I told him, "and then I fell in."

I turned to face this man, waiting for him to laugh. Everyone laughs at this story. But my father's face was stone.

"I was there."

His words hung in the starry air like threads of time.

I remember, I told him, a fountain. In a big space, maybe indoors. I remember walking along the edge, the rippling water sparkling under my feet. I must have held my arms out like a tightrope walker, balancing between one world and another.

And then, I told him, I fell. I tipped over, one of those falls where one moment you are upright and the next you're in the water, soaked through like a prehistoric amphibian, your black hair matted to your head and your clothes floating. I was scared. I didn't tell him how scared I was in those moments before someone lifted me out of the water.

A red-checkered tablecloth. A waiter wrapped me in a red-checkered tablecloth. I sat on my mother's lap, cuddled close to her as I was warmed, relieved of my fear and surprise and embarrassment.

"I was there," he said again. "It was at the Black Forest Inn." It was eerie to hear him speak with such authority about a time from my childhood. He had always been an imaginary father, the one I knew existed but had no memory of. And now, here he was, telling me something about my own life, something he knew and I didn't. "A German restaurant. We liked to go there, your mom and me and Dick and Sally. There was a courtyard with a small fountain. Do you remember that restaurant? Is it still there? Shit." He spoke in English, his accent still peppered with American colloquialisms from the 1970s. "It was a great place to drink German beer."

Even though his body was still next to me on a bench in Cali, Colombia, I could see that in his mind he was once again drinking beer with my mother and her parents in a restaurant in Minneapolis. The echo of falling water in the blackness sounded vast and forgiving. He rolled the cigarette between his thumb and forefinger and then cupped his hand around the match. The phosphoric smell rose as the flame lit, and I was suddenly chilled by the night air.

"You fell in."

I began to calculate. It must have been a time when he and my mother were still married and we were still an approximation of a family. There is a small window of time when all this could have happened, shortly before talk of divorce, perhaps even days, minutes before. I try to picture myself as part of a little family with a mother and a father and a baby girl. We would have been dressed like hippies, I would have been wearing something hand-sewn and sturdy shoes to help me walk steadily, something that gave me the confidence to balance on that ledge. I couldn't have been more than a year or two.

■ ■ ■

I have no memories of my father. People used to ask me, "What is it like not having a dad?" I never knew how to answer them. What is it like living on the moon? What is it like having three hands? These are unimaginable things, preposterous even. "Don't you miss having a father?" they would ask. I longed to say, Don't you miss being an astronaut? And they would answer, I don't know, I've never been an astronaut. And I would say, Exactly.

With no memories of my father, how could I be sure he was ever there? Now, here was the proof. That memory, that connection. In the form of a fountain. The possibility that my memories coincided with his.

But I know that memories can be tricky and fluid, can fade in and out and transmute themselves. We can take over other people's memories, shape them with repeated recitations, mold them until they suit our needs. Our own memories are just as easily manipulated and kneaded and refined from internal or external forces until they are either further or closer to the truth. It is possible—probable even—that I have been told the story of falling into the fountain so many times that I only think I remember it, that it isn't a memory but a story.

I said this to my father, and he nodded. We listened to the water rushing over the marble in front of us.

"But I remember the red-checkered tablecloth," I said. I remembered it so clearly I could feel the overwashed cotton and smell the chlorine soaking into the cloth.

"It *was* a red-checkered tablecloth," he confirmed.

"No one would have told me a detail like that. People don't say, 'And then you were wrapped in a red-checkered tablecloth.'"

He exhaled smoke into the night air, contemplating this.

"Do they?"

"They probably don't."

I looked over at him. He said little; he didn't process through words. I was afraid my sequence of spiral thinking might have pushed his English comprehension to the brink. But I couldn't stop talking. My words tumbled out, one after another, falling.

"It isn't the kind of detail you tell people, at least not over and over. And I would have had to hear that story over and over again so that I would internalize it enough to make it feel like a memory. It must be a memory. I was there and I remember."

I saw the orange end of his cigarette light the darkness. Perhaps he was still in Minnesota with his first wife, drawing on a pint of Spaten.

"I remember," I repeated, more to myself than to him. "I remember that red-checkered tablecloth."

He finished his cigarette, and I watched it roll across the sidewalk. I could tell that he didn't understand what this meant to me. I had no childhood memories of him, but I remembered a moment, and he was in that moment, and I felt like I really was his daughter, like I really was born of a mother and a father, and that my father came from Colombia, and by some twist of fate he found himself with a daughter in a German restaurant in Minnesota, and the daughter fell in a fountain, and there was his wife swaddling their baby in a red-checkered tablecloth.

"So do I," he said, squeezing my hand.

We stood up and walked past the fountain. Arm in arm again, we crossed the deserted plaza until the sound of our footsteps moving forward drowned out the falling water behind us.

10

MY FATHER TALKED AND TOLD ME NOTHING, he showed me photographs and explained none of them, he embraced me but somehow kept his distance. He wanted to keep me at arm's length and yet close. When Ceci wanted to take me and her niece María Fernanda to the hot springs at the Termales de Coconuco, he was reluctant to let me go.

"We'll be back tonight," Ceci had cajoled, soothing him like a woman accustomed to the job.

"Be careful," he said as if he had a right to say that.

I was relieved to get away from my moody father for the day; three days of travel to Cali with him had been exhausting, as was being his daughter. And the hot springs were as breathtaking as Ceci had promised they would be. The small, natural pool known as the Aguas Tibias—lukewarm water—was crystalline. Fed by a mountain hot spring, the water was blue, and the little pool was rimmed with the ferns and grasses of the mountainside. It was beautiful—and it was much colder than we had been led to believe.

"¡Qué frío!" María Fernanda said, laughing with blue lips.

"I'm freezing!" I cried, my teeth chattering.

"You don't want to go to the Aguas Hirviendas, do you?" Ceci asked from where she stood, warm, fully clothed, and out of the water.

Hirvienda means "boiling." It sounded better to me, and I nodded.

"But that's where all the crowds are," she reminded us.

Despite the prospect of crowds, María Fernanda and I were eager for somewhere warmer. It was late afternoon by now, and we were chilled and tired.

"I have an idea," Ceci said as she drove the Suzuki farther into the mountains to the Aguas Hirviendas and the light began to fade from the sky, "Let's stay overnight here. The Coconuco Hotel is wonderful. We'll get a room, and then we can go to the Termales."

I knew my father wouldn't like this idea. He had been anxious at the prospect of letting me out of his sight for this trip up the mountain, as if he still saw me as a child who needed protection and watching. Something that, I thought with sudden irritation, he should have thought of a long time ago, long before I was a twenty-one-year-old adult.

"Let's do it," I said.

By the time we had settled into the hotel and changed back into damp bathing suits, it was dark. At the Termales de Coconuco, the natural *aguas hirviendas* that bubbled up from the earth boiled our skin raw and made sweat drip down our faces. Streetlights lined the park and cast a bluish glow over the scene of revelers. We passed by tubs filled with couples soaking in the boiling water and skirted by the slides crawling with children still awake after their bedtimes. We tracked down three plastic cups and a bottle of rum and headed for the last pool, one that was empty of both tourists and water. Even though it was late evening, the pool was just filling with water pouring in through jets near what would become the deep end. We descended a ladder to the pool's floor and splashed and kicked, holding our cups aloft to prevent spills.

"Who wants another?" Ceci asked. She climbed the ladder and refilled the plastic cups with rum and Coke, which waited for us at the pool's edge. Then back down she climbed, rear end first in her floral one-piece.

We sang songs, we danced, we teased, me in my half-American, half-Colombian, Spain-influenced Spanish. We were nighttime nymphs, wingless fairies, drunken sprites. And while we played like children in the bottom of that pool, I wondered how I ended up here. How did I end up in the middle of a war-torn South American country with two strangers, dancing in my swimming suit at ten o'clock on a January night? How do we end up anywhere?

"Don't tell Renzo we gave you rum!" Ceci cried, and María Fernanda collapsed in giggles. In Colombia, rum is pronounced *ron,* and that made me laugh all over again, pushing aside thoughts of this man Renzo, my father.

As the pool filled, I lay back in the water. I felt weightless, floating and looking up at the shadowing slopes and black skies above. The mountains of that region of the Andes rise to ten thousand feet and higher, and perhaps my breathing became shallow. The thin air, combined with the *ron,* made all of us feel even more drunk.

The next morning, Ceci took a meandering route back down the mountain, and at midday we stopped on the side of the road near a little stream. The mountainside was steep and grass covered, like most of the landscape at this altitude. The almost vertical slopes were shocking in their formations, so different from any kinds of mountains I had seen before. Huge leaves provided shade, and jagged gray rocks jutted here and there as if meant for climbing and exploring. Thin clouds obscured the sun, and the air smelled like dust and rotting leaves. Ceci and María Fernanda pulled out the Cokes and the bottle of rum again. I took my camera and walked along the road a way, taking pictures of the hillside and of a brown cow that grazed at a precarious incline.

"Look at us!" María Fernanda shouted.

I looked up, and there they were. Ceci had rolled back the plastic and canvas cover of the Suzuki, and they were standing on the back seat of the car grinning at me. Their heads and shoulders and their hands holding the rum and Cokes protruded from the open roof.

"Say *whiskey*!" I said and snapped a picture, capturing that scene for myself to remember later.

Near the Suzuki, we found a bridge by the stream, and I taught María Fernanda and Ceci to play a game called "Poohsticks." I had learned about this game from *Winnie-the-Pooh,* read to me by my grandfather on snowy nights in Minnesota. Poohsticks is a very simple game: you lean over a bridge and drop a stick into the water, just a little one. You watch the moving water take hold of your twig and carry it away until it slips under the wooden boards of the bridge. Quick! someone yells, and you all rush to the other side of the bridge, lean over—way over—and watch for your stick to reappear. Sometimes it takes so long, you're sure you'll never see your little twig again, you're sure it's caught on something, it's swirling in an infinity of whirling water. And then it suddenly bobs up again. You feel proud, even though you had nothing to do with its progress.

María Fernanda and Ceci had never heard of Poohsticks, and whether it was the afternoon *tragos* of rum or the absurdity of the competition, these two Colombian women embraced it. There might have been guerrillas in those hills watching our game; perhaps trucks carrying arms and drugs hurtled past the Suzuki. But if they did, we didn't notice. The three of us ran back and forth across a little bridge in the middle of the Colombian Andes breathless with laughter.

And just for a moment, I didn't wonder how I ended up there. I didn't wonder about all the things that didn't happen or all the things that did. I just dropped in my little twig and laughed at the ridiculousness of the game, the idiocy, the wonderful pointlessness of it all.

When we arrived home red-cheeked with an empty bottle, my father exclaimed, "You let her drink rum!"

"Renzo, querido," Ceci soothed, "she's a Colombiana."

"You have to be careful," Renzo said, his words slurring from the bottle of something he had opened while we were gone. The alcohol made him even more emotional than usual, made him overcompensate for years of missed parenting. He was lonely, I saw, but I held my mouth in a straight line. And I saw something else in his face, a darkness in his eyes; the fact that I was twenty-one and fully adult, fully American, did not seem possible to him, I supposed. I had been absent, and now I had appeared again—a lifetime for me, a moment for him.

"Anika, my dear," he said, reaching for me, putting his arm around my shoulder in a protective embrace. All he had left, I supposed, was to shield me from the harmless, from *tragos* of rum on a mountain road. That there were other things from which a parent might protect a child either did not occur to him or were too numerous to comprehend.

11

A WEEK OR SO INTO MY VISIT, my father helped me place an international phone call to my boyfriend. He asked what Dave's family thought of my visit to Colombia, and I told him they conflated Mexico with every other South American country.

"Tell them we eat bananas," my father said, laughing at his own joke. "Tell them we gave you a nice tree to sleep in." When I hung up the phone, my father said, "Never marry a Latino." He was speaking from experience; he knew Latinos like him did not make good husbands.

Before getting swept off her feet, my mother once told her father: "I'm so glad you raised me the way you did. I would never let a man sweep me off my feet." Despite this burgeoning feminism, she was the product of American popular culture in the mid-twentieth century, a reader of Daphne du Maurier and Margaret Mitchell. So it wasn't really her fault that when she arrived in Colombia, she became a new person. She was without her parents, her brothers, her routine of the mundane. Her facility with Spanish perhaps gave her a confidence she had lacked before, and when she saw this man, this dark and exotic man, I wonder if she pictured a romance novel, a film, a happily-ever-after. Perhaps they were each other's fairy tales come to life.

My mother arrived home from her extended stay in Colombia, and on the way from the airport she told my grandfather that she was getting married. My grandfather tells me it remains the worst moment of his life. His only daughter. Age nineteen and she was leaving him. He was certain he would never see her again.

But before she left, the couple had a Christmastime wedding at the family's large Congregational church in Minneapolis. The smaller chapel, not the sanctuary, had been reserved, and my mother wore an orange blouse and flowered skirt. My father wore necklaces of beads, and they exchanged rings that were really spoon handles curved into circles. A friend of theirs played Bob Dylan (*Lay, lady, lay, lay across my big brass bed*...), and I'm sure my great-grandmother was appalled. No one said anything, though, and the guests ate wedding cake. My uncle and his band played rock and roll in the basement of my grandparents' house. Was this an auspicious start, that church wedding and Bob Dylan?

The honeymoon was a family affair: my mother's parents and Ginny and the newlyweds at the family's northern Minnesota cabin. Snow and cold. My father painted in white and shadows. There is a photograph from that week at the snowy cabin. My mother and father are cocooned together on a little sofa, her arms wrapped around him. My mother looks up at the camera, a pout on her lips. At first glance, it seems that my father is studying her hands with adoration. Look closer, though, and he is actually studying his own hands, those artist's hands. At the end of the honeymoon, Renzo fell ill, and my grandparents paid his hospital bills, and my mother nursed him. He had a long history of stomach-related health issues, and he has always been good at playing the patient.

They didn't have an apartment in Minnesota at first. They didn't have much. They lived with my grandparents, who were always taking in strays. My grandparents hosted foreign exchange students, refugees from Tibet, and their own errant and wandering children.

I imagine the people who became my mom and dad as the young lovers you might see in a film's montage of romance. Corny music appropriate to the era plays (*I am as constant as a northern star*...), swells in the background, and I watch my parents go about their doomed lives (*You may say that I'm a dreamer*...). Here goes my father, on the bus to the College of Art and Design—paid for by his in-laws (*I've seen fire and I've seen rain*...). My mother, a scarf on her head and bell-bottoms swaying, takes the bus the other direction, to the University of Minnesota—paid for by her parents (*You've just got to see me through another day . . .*). What music plays when they go and ask my grandparents for money? What is the soundtrack for the arguments they had over when to return to my father's homeland? How soon into their marriage did things begin to show wear?

It was all love and passion. Or maybe just passion. Or maybe not enough passion. Renzo was an artist, a bohemian. He had been abandoned by his parents, separated from his siblings. He had been sent away to upstate New York for high school, something that was both transformative and stifling. He was both selfish and selfless. His ego was both huge and trampled. He loved his young American wife, but there were so many pretty women.

Keeping house in Colombia was complicated and frustrating for a Minnesota girl. There were in-laws and cockroaches and late nights alone in foreign apartments. How could my mother have a life there, where she had no family, where everything was exotic? Perhaps this was when she began to think that the adventure had gone on too long.

Keeping house in a rented duplex in Minneapolis with no phone and no car was difficult. This wasn't the life my mother had imagined. She expected something, but even she didn't know what. And now Renzo was unhappy, homesick. They wandered the art galleries; artists will seek beauty, will tell themselves they are entitled to beauty, they need beauty. The muse, the inspiration. Temptation was everywhere.

A baby, they thought, would fix everything. A baby. A baby to bind them together. They moved back to Colombia, lived in a small house in a small village called Silvia, and made a baby. In Silvia, they not only had no phone and no car, they also had no heat.

A few months into the pregnancy, unable or unwilling to talk about her unhappiness, Nancy fled. She went back to the sweltering humidity of Cali, back to where all these adventures had begun. She was back in the valley city, this time with a growing belly, a permanent tie to Colombia. She left Renzo behind in Silvia, removed the ring from her swollen finger. She bumped around the city in tentlike maternity muumuus and lived with friends in an apartment in Cali. She shared a room with Beth, an American who worked in Silvia a few times a week.

"Never marry a Latino," my father repeated. He patted my leg before stepping into the courtyard for a cigarette. "Marry Dave."

12

EVEN THOUGH I DIDN'T SEE MY FATHER in the five years after that visit to Colombia, I did eventually marry Dave. It was a summer wedding at a city park in Minnesota. My mother walked me down the makeshift aisle, our fingers entwined. An invitation to my father had been sent too late for him to either accept or decline, and so he called during the reception while my friends and family drank and ate and laughed. The stars were out as my father congratulated me over the phone, his voice distorted by the distance.

Besides that wedding call, our sole communication became the emails my father wrote whenever he felt like it, sporadic and whimsical as that was. Like the foreign airmail envelopes that used to arrive when I was a child, these correspondences often felt like they were sent not only across political and geographical boundaries but across time, too.

He wrote to me in simple, adoring words as if I were still the baby he remembered. He attached scanned black and white photographs of my mother when she was twenty or baby pictures of me in his arms or his own artwork in bold colors with sharply defined lines. Once he emailed a scanned poster he had designed for a children's relief fund. *This is you,* he wrote in the email. The stylized photograph shows a little brown-haired girl with blunt-cut bangs and round cheeks. In the corner of the poster, a date is written in pencil in my father's square print: *1972.* Two years before I was born. My new husband, ever the pragmatist, concluded that he had gotten the date wrong, but I ended up feeling a little off-balance and uncertain as to what was true and what was not.

The day my inbox revealed the most memorable of all his enig-matic emails, a breeze, smelling faintly of garlic from the fields of Gil-roy in the next valley, wafted through the window of our California apartment. In 2001, email was, even in Silicon Valley, still a fairly novel method of communication and was primarily conducted through the likes of Yahoo! and AOL. Google was in its infancy, and Netscape was still a viable option for browsing the nascent World Wide Web. Most people (and everyone in Colombia) still connected to the inter-net by noisy modems and clumsy phone lines. The infrastructure—everything, actually—was antiquated in Popayán, and the internet connection was slow and intermittent. Sending emails was a deliber-ate affair requiring planning and consideration, time and preparation. But how much forethought, I now wonder, went into this message? Had he carefully crafted his subject line and fine-tuned the first para-graph? Or had he simply, in a few impulsive moments, dashed off the words that would change my life so completely?

This was what I wondered when I saw the subject line of his email: *Brother.*

My mother has three brothers. My father had a brother, my uncle—whom I had never met. My grandmother had two older brothers she adored, and my grandfather had an older brother he never got along with. My husband is the middle between two brothers, with whom he has nothing in common. But I grew up an only child, the sun around which my mother—and often my maternal grandparents—orbited.

For most of my life, my family was just the two of us, a complete unit, and I came to see my world as a yin and yang: mother and daugh-ter, the two of us forging a path during a time when the phenomenon of the single mother was new. In the 1980s, only one in ten children was raised by a single parent, and those (mostly) women were often vilified for their single status, seen as freeloaders or welfare moms. Other neighborhood kids in our mostly blue-collar apartment com-plex had single mothers, but those children also had dads somewhere, men they would visit for a few weeks in the summer or every other weekend.

But to me, family meant that simple dyad: a mother and a daughter. This was interrupted briefly during the five years my mother was married to her second husband and I found myself with a stepfather and two unruly stepbrothers. But even their existence was fleeting; after her second divorce, I went back to my rightful spot, center of the universe, an only child.

I looked at the subject line of my father's email in the filtered California sunlight of our second bedroom, which served as an office. During my visit to Colombia five years before, I had asked Ceci if she wanted to have children. We were in the kitchen preparing food for a New Year's Eve celebration at her parents' house in the center of Popayán. Ceci was almost twenty years younger than my father (closer in age to me than to him), and the way she bustled around had seemed so maternal.

"I had several miscarriages," she had told me as she stirred dessert, a lemon mousse made with the lemons from the back courtyard squeezed one by one until the juice covered our hands.

"I'm sorry," I said, although at twenty-one I had no idea what that meant, what it felt like to either want or lose a child. "Maybe someday," I said brightly.

"Maybe," she had said.

The leaves of a Japanese maple rustled outside my window, and the traffic on the expressway behind our apartment droned. My inbox, with its message from my father, waited.

I clicked to open the email and read the first line: *You don't know this.*

That there was something I didn't know came as no surprise. It would be easier to count the things I did know about my father than those I didn't. I knew he was the grandson of Italian immigrants to Colombia, that he was born in the 1940s, the older brother of fraternal twins, who trailed after him. I knew his life hadn't been as shrouded in tragedy and miracles as the characters in a Gabriel García Márquez story, but there were still mysteries. I knew he had been sent to the United States for high school and college, but I didn't know what that had done to him. I knew he married and later divorced my mother, but I didn't know what had happened. I knew there were secrets but didn't even know enough to ask about them. I had heard stories, seen photographs, studied the archival evidence, but without growing up with this man in my life, could I ever know him? Even after I went to Colombia and met the man who was my father, the things I didn't know about him—about this half of my family and about the country where I was born—could be lined up and stretched from California to South America and back again.

I stared at the computer monitor and stretched my palms flat against the cool, fake wood of the ridiculously large desk we had chosen for the office. It had barely fit through the doors of the apartment but had seemed proof that we were here in California to stay. The computer's CPU hummed. From the living room, I could hear Dave and my grandparents talking, my grandfather's storytelling drone punctuated by my grandmother's near-deaf contributions. They were visiting us en route from Minnesota to Hawaii, had traveled by RV, and would then catch a flight at SFO. I had escaped the socializing for a moment to check my email, ostensibly because I was in graduate school but really because I was slightly homesick for Minnesota and craved any connection to my old life.

You don't know this, I read in my father's email, *but you have a brother.*

My eyes moved down the screen.

There was an address. An address not far from our apartment. A quick jaunt down the 280. My breath came faster and shallower. There was a name. Renzo. The same name as my father. I could still hear the mumble of conversation in the next room, but a sound like ocean waves in my ears was roaring. An adult brother. In the United States.

The sun sliced through the window, an irritant to my eyes, which were suddenly stinging.

Brother.

And then I was standing in the living room where the three of them—Dave, my grandmother, my grandfather—were lined up on the couch, that same couch where we had agreed to get married a year earlier, the same couch that we had picked out in Berkeley but that had been delivered late when it had fallen off the delivery truck. I wondered if we had received a replacement couch or if they had repaired this one. You never really know the provenance of things outside your line of vision.

Dave and my grandparents watched me hyperventilate.

"I have—" I gasped as if I were at high altitude in air depleted of oxygen. They stared at me, unable to guess what I was trying to say.

"I have—" I tried again. I felt like a caricature of a human, like Saturday morning cartoons.

"I have a brother."

Dave was the first one to move. He stood up, and a bag materialized into which I breathed for several moments. The rough paper, as brown and wrinkled as my father's skin, rattled with each breath. My grandparents didn't say much. They knew the stories were complicated.

13

THE QUICK, SHALLOW INTAKES OF BREATH typical of hyperventilation saturate the body with oxygen—too much of a good thing. The paper bag, I learned later, helps to even out the carbon dioxide in the blood. The next day, after my grandparents had returned to their RV, I thumbed through my old address book searching for the country code and meaningless digits that would connect my father's world to mine. I almost never called him. First it was because I didn't have a phone number, then I blamed it on the cost of long-distance phone calls. Once I had phoned after news reports of an earthquake near his city of Popayán, but he had been fine, and I hadn't called again. Until now.

I entered in the country code and the string of numbers. On the rare occasions that he contacted me, Ceci generally placed the call. I would first speak in Spanish with a Colombian operator, who would say my name with her fluid accent, then I would be connected with the tinny voice of Ceci rattling off something to the operator, who would leave the line. Ceci put my father on the phone.

"My dear," he said, his voice expectant.

I told him I had received his email.

"He wants to meet you," my father said.

He. Despite having a name and an address, I couldn't really comprehend a person who would be given the title of brother.

I thought of my unruly stepbrothers and the first summer we had lived in our house. They had taught me to play baseball with ghost runners. I was thirteen, a *Little Women* and *Anne of Green Gables* kind of girl, and knew nothing about baseball and even less about brothers.

They had led me out into the vast backyard of our new joint home, where a tall pine tree called to me to be climbed. One of my stepbrothers had the fat plastic bat, the other a couple of orange plastic cones for bases. The late-summer sunset slanted through the climbing tree's branches, and a few mosquitoes made their presence known. The grass needed cutting (a job my stepfather would eventually delegate to me, one of the countless reasons to despise him) and scratched my ankles when I swung at the Wiffle ball. I was two and four years older than they were, but they could each hit with more accuracy than I ever could or would.

"You hit," the older one explained to me, "and run to first base."

The younger one stepped in front of his older brother and in the process got closer to me than I liked. "If you don't get out," he interrupted, his voice quick and high-pitched with excitement, "your ghost runner holds your place at the base and you hit again."

The older one jostled for his place back, impatient to begin. "Okay? Got it?"

Having never been to a baseball game or even watched one on TV, I didn't really get it. My mother had had the luxury as a single parent to introduce me only to the things she cared about. I had gone to folk festivals and art museums. I often went along with her to see Garrison Keillor's live radio show *A Prairie Home Companion,* long before it became a national institution. I trailed behind her as she explored art fairs, and I obligingly studied animals in the zoo. We spent weekends at her parents' cabin on a lake in northern Minnesota, where she taught me how to paddle a canoe and jump off a dock. But she never took me to arenas or stadiums or tuned into broadcast games on summer evenings.

But I loved the idea of ghost runners—that there was a spirit out there who could take your place if needed, stand in for you, help you get ahead and win the game. Maybe ghosts are more appealing to only children, who are so accustomed to being alone. Ghosts were perhaps an extension of the affinity I had developed for companions I couldn't see.

The sun sank lower as the three of us ran around in circles chasing our ghosts. I almost always missed the ball and was constantly in the outfield. From that position I was free to let my mind wander, to watch the cardinal that flitted to the top of the pine tree, to listen to the muffled laughter of neighbor children in other backyards.

"Your ghost runner is out!" one of my stepbrothers shouted at the other. As I came in from the outfield, I could see three big welts from mosquito bites on his face and neck.

"Is not!" the other screamed back, leaning forward in an attempt to amplify his voice in anger before slamming the plastic bat on the ground.

"Is too!" The other kicked second base out of alignment until it was more like one-and-a-quarter base, and the game ended for real when they both went stomping back into the house.

I stood in the pink light of dusk, slapping mosquitoes, an only child with no one but the ghost runners for company.

"He didn't talk to me for a long time," my father said when I asked why he had never told me about this brother.

I stood in the middle of the living room, where the relentless sun beat down. The roof of our apartment building was uninsulated, and in the heat of late spring the furniture in the apartment felt warm to the touch as if it had been sitting outside. I laid a hand on the back of the futon couch and let the warmth soak into my palm while my other hand gripped the cordless phone. I could feel my teeth clenching and my tongue pushing against them. A thick and angry saliva gathered in my mouth, and I could barely murmur, "But why didn't you tell me?"

"I thought I had lost him forever."

In the hollowness of the long-distance call, my father explained that this person had stopped corresponding with him around the same time I had sent my first letter. In the echoes of his voice, I could hear the choice I had made as a teenager reverberating into the future that was now my present.

"That's why I didn't tell you."

I was silent. This was not the answer I was looking for.

"But now we can all be family again."

"What about my mom? Did she know?"

"Nancy knew," he said, without missing a beat.

I said nothing. I knew she wouldn't lie to me. I knew no such thing about my father.

My father put Ceci on the line.

"You know," she said in Spanish to me. It was a statement, a fact.

"I know."

Then Ceci spewed a rush of words that with the distortions of the phone call and my rusty Spanish I thought I misunderstood.

"¿Qué dijiste?" I asked, confused.

She repeated: "Now we can be a happy family!"

I thought of Ceci longing for a baby, getting another adult child instead. I thought of her handling her Suzuki jeep like a race car driver, handling the rest of us with just as much aplomb.

After I hung up, the words in my father's email duplicated behind my eyes the way looking at the sun can produce its replica everywhere you look. They swirled around my head like a preposterous cyclone. I paced the apartment and finally collapsed into the desk chair in the office, twitched in my seat. Was my life a lie, then? What was truth? What was reality? The chair began to rotate. My father repeated the name (the same as his!), explained nothing over and over while all the time I wondered. I could hardly tell whether it was the chair spinning or my world. Did I really have a brother? Did my mother know? Did I exist? And still the goddamn birds chirped outside the window, and the California sun shone.

14

I WASN'T SURE THAT I WANTED TO KNOW the answers, but the next day I called my mother. I lay across the bed on my stomach, propped up on my elbows, and dialed my mother's number, one that could have been mine if I hadn't chosen to move to California, hadn't married Dave, hadn't lived the life I was living. I knew something that I didn't know before. Something, I was beginning to understand, other people did. It had begun to gnaw at me in the night—had my mother known about this brother? Had she also lied to me? How deep did these secrets go, and where did they stop?

"You need to sit down. Are you sitting down?" I asked her. "I got an email from Renzo."

My mother, on the rare occasions that she talked about him, always referred to him as Renzo, never "your father." And without siblings to discuss him with, it was easier to refer to him by his first name. After all, for many years the concept of father was quite abstract. It was a word, nothing more.

"I got an email," I said, "that says I have a brother."

There was a pause, a silence that felt as vast as the distance between California and Minnesota.

"Did you know that?" I asked.

In that unspoken space, I could feel my life taking another turn. It reminded me of the time my mother and I had sat (inexplicably) on the floor of the bathroom in the first house she bought. I was twelve at the time, and she had explained that she was getting married, that we would move, changing my life's course. And then again when, six years later, when I was a senior in high school, we sat on the carpeted stairs (again, the floor) and she told me she was getting a divorce, shifting my life yet again.

"Wow." That was my mother's response.

I explained everything I had learned from Renzo. That the boy's name was also Renzo, that the mother's name was Beth. And then it was my mother's turn to explain to me that almost as soon as she found out she was pregnant with me, a choice that had been a poorly thought-out plan to repair their marriage, she had left Renzo for the first time.

"We weren't getting along, so I moved to Cali. He stayed in Silvia."

Silvia is a little village about ten miles from Popayán founded, co-incidentally (or not), on my birthday in 1562. The town in the Cordillera Central of the Andes is populated mainly by the Guambiano Indians, who live on a reservation higher up in the mountains. The Guambianos are artisans and farmers, weaving beautiful tapestries and growing crops that can withstand the Andean terrain. My father had told me that they were one of the few groups legally allowed to grow coca, that they chew on the leaves to counteract high-altitude symptoms. My parents had lived for a time among the Guambianos and the Colombians descended from colonial Spaniards. They lived in a rundown adobe house that had no heat or running water, and I don't know whether coca leaves helped them tolerate their lives. My father ran a small factory there that produced his artisan wooden toys and carved ducks.

"Beth was my roommate in Cali," my mother said. "She was nice. I crashed with her and a couple other American friends. Beth had work in Silvia, so she was up there a lot."

I tried to imagine my mother, pregnant with me, sharing an apartment with hippie girls and watching one of them travel to the town where her husband was.

"I knew they slept together."

There are many things about our parents that we don't want to know. I thought of the first day I awoke in Cali, in Ceci's sister's apartment, on my trip five years earlier. The night before had been a blur of Spanish and the *besos* and *abrazos* from Ceci's relatives. I had spent the night in the hard twin bed of one of Ceci's nephews, the unfamiliar and scratchy sheets tangled in the tropical heat. In the morning, I walked through the open door into the room where Ceci and my father had slept.

"Anika, my dear," my father had cried, a large cup of coffee in his hands and a bigger smile on his face.

And I froze. Ceci was in white pajamas on the bed. My father was on a makeshift mattress on the floor below her. He sat amid the rumpled blankets in nothing but brown men's bikini briefs. He was skinny with a sunken belly. My mother had told me that he had had part of his stomach removed when he was a teenager, a remedy for chronic ulcers that the doctors then had elected to remove rather than treat. His illnesses and the resulting complications had made him somewhat delicate, she had told me. And skinny. And naked.

"My dear," he said again, patting the sheets next to him, "come here. Have you had coffee?"

I didn't know what to say or do. I tried not to be embarrassed at my father's nakedness; he was my father, after all. But there were things I didn't want to know about him.

"I knew they slept together," my mother repeated across the distance, "but I didn't know Beth got pregnant."

I slid to the floor and sat with my back leaning against the bed frame, staring at the shoes on the floor in the closet, the blossoms of dust caught in the runners of the sliding doors, the Post-It note stuck under the leg of the nightstand. I gripped the receiver like a life ring.

I don't know what else I said or how we left things that first time, but I remember that she said, "It was the seventies. You know that song? 'Love the One You're With'? That's how it was back then."

This did not comfort me.

15

I COULDN'T BE ANGRY WITH MY MOTHER, and I couldn't be angry with a person that, at this point, might not even exist, the brother I had never known about. But I could be angry with my father.

The birthday parties, the Christmases, the summer vacations. I began to seethe. I pictured myself walking down the aisle of my graduation ceremony, at my wedding. All those significant moments as an only child. Was my life a lie, then? What was truth? What was reality? Angry, I thought. I was angry.

Before hanging up, my father had said, "He can't wait to meet you, my dear."

He.

"Tell him I'm not ready to meet him," I had said. I enunciated each word, my voice already raised to be heard across the international phone lines. "Tell him that."

I thought of that lonely trip to Colombia.

How could this have been kept a secret? The existence of a brother. My brother.

"I told Renzo I wasn't ready to talk to him yet," I said to Dave as we sat together on the futon.

"That's good. Wait until you're ready."

Dave reached for my hand across the mattress, which was already growing lumpy from so many overnight guests. We had been in California for almost five years by now, and our friends and families liked to use our apartment as a free vacation spot.

"I'm not ready," I said again.

"I know."

He knew a lot. My marriage was the opposite of my parents', who had barely known one another when they got married. Dave and I had been together for years, since we were children, really. We were eighteen when we fell in love the summer of the Great Midwest Flood of 1993, an apt beginning I now think. The Mississippi River had endured record amounts of rain that spring, and as tributaries over-flowed their banks, rodents drowned in their nests, baby rabbits were left for dead, and sapling trees choked to death. The rains beat down, saturating the soil from Minnesota to Ohio. The raging waters dam-aged houses and crops, displaced bystanders, and disrupted life. The water washed out paths and roadways, leaving behind a film of mud and muck, a high-water line to mark the occasion.

I remember sitting in Dave's car one night, his hand reaching for mine across the emergency brake. We had spent the day along the flooded riverbanks. Dave had hauled our bikes to the park, and I watched his sinewy arms as he unloaded the car. I pedaled after him down muddy trails bumpy with the intruding root systems of poplar and maple. We biked through brush and puddles, splattering our shirts with muck while the flooded trunks of trees stood firm in the water like bathers afraid to take the plunge. Then the topography sharpened, undulating into ups and downs, until I found myself following him down a steep turn, rocks and fallen branches rattling my tires. I was afraid, but I trusted him. Peddling behind him, I watched his long, thin figure strain and push. The wind whipping at his T-shirt exposed his pale back, a sight that seemed somehow slightly provocative and im-mensely endearing.

At the last curve, he reached the bottom first and stopped to watch my progress. With his eyes on me, I lost control on the incline and went down. As I fell, I watched him watching me. He stood at the bottom of the hill, straddling his bike, coated in dirt, a scrape on his hand brilliant red with fresh-drawn blood. I tumbled down faster than my bike, and his toppled as he lurched toward me, trying to catch me.

His hands had been warm on my thigh as he inspected my skinned knee. We touched under the pretense of emergency; I took his hand

and placed my arm around his neck for support. He was solid and real, and his careful attention made me feel protected, even with a bleeding kneecap. We sat in the dirt and drank from the same water bottle, the spout touching both our lips.

I want to say it was raining that night when we were parked outside the apartment my mother had rented after her second divorce. The wind battered the car until we were blown together. It was the summer after high school, and she had taught me that men could be dangerous and unpredictable, that they could hurt you and control you and stifle you. But I was old enough—or maybe young enough—to know that mothers could be wrong. A torrent of fireflies (or maybe just raindrops) poured down on the windshield, until the droplets of reflected light were washed away with a swish of wiper blades. Lightning streaks made patterns across the sky and made maps of our life to come, brought us to that moment.

Later that summer, as the sun tried to dry out the earth, Dave and I brought a picnic to a meadow well above the floodplains, where the purple loosestrife scratched our legs and ankles as we waded through it. We stretched out on a wool blanket, the prairie grasses flowing around our island, and held on to each other. And seven years later when we got married in a grassy clearing at a park next to the Mississippi, there were no floods or lightning strikes.

The rings we exchanged that day were both beautiful and practical, the ruby on mine set deep to prevent any loss or catching, and his a simple band. A ring is a symbol of marriage because its infinite loop is meant to be a metaphor of your unending love. The morning after the wedding, lying in bed at the hotel, I twisted mine around my finger, thinking of the rings at the bottom of my mother's jewelry box. She and my father had worn rings that were spoon handles bent into interesting but finite curves, each ending in a flourish of silverwork. For her second marriage, my mother and stepfather had chosen puzzle rings, gold bands that intertwined artfully and yet could easily become undone until all that was left was a jumble of metal under the necklaces and earrings she no longer wore. With one final twist of my own wedding ring, I climbed out of bed and put on a luxurious hotel robe. I was standing at the window looking down at the Minnesota summer morning when I heard a clatter from the bathroom where Dave was taking a shower.

"I accidentally washed my ring off," he said, coming out of the bathroom with a white towel around his waist. Dave's ring, it turned out, had not fallen down the drain. We had luck or fate on our side; no hotel concierge or plumber was necessary. He had plucked the ring from the soapy water at the bottom of the tub and placed it back on his finger. An opposing phase of the moon, a different tilt of the planet, and everything could have been different. Each moment there is the possibility of the split between alternatives, realities that can be shifted.

The phone call, I suppose, was inevitable. But when I heard a voice identifying himself as Renzo, I slid to the floor of the galley kitchen, where I could see grains of uncooked rice caught between the vinyl flooring and trim.

"I'm sorry," I told this other Renzo, this Renzo who was my half brother. "I told my dad I wasn't ready to talk to you."

The words *my dad* sat there, silent but not unnoticed.

"Oh."

"Didn't he tell you that?"

"No, he didn't."

There was a pause during which I played with the coiled phone cord, let it bounce and sway like a suspension bridge.

"Would you like to meet?"

"I need to think about it," I said, and I felt like I was breaking some-one's heart.

Perhaps as much of a coward as my father, I tested the water of frater-nity by dipping a toe into email correspondence as if I were afraid the voice and meeting would make the whole thing real, as if I could keep reality at bay by typing out my questions.

Where do you live? I asked this brother of mine through impersonal bits and bytes.

By coincidence or fate, he lived so near my apartment in California that we could have seen each other at the grocery store, a reggae concert, a red light. I tried to think whether I had ever seen a young man and thought he could be related to me. I began to study every stranger on the street, wondering if that person was family. The world felt simultaneously bigger and smaller. All relations seemed strangely ephemeral, objects appeared impermanent, my own emotions wavered along all segments of the spectrum, everything beginning to feel as surreal as if Colombia's magic had followed me.

How old are you?
Twenty-six.
When's your birthday?
March.

I have never been a mathematical whiz, but even I could calculate that we were mere months apart, that he was conceived at a time when I was still a zygote hidden beneath my mother's peasant blouse. She would have barely been showing the bump that would be me at that time, when two women, carrying Renzo's seed, crossed paths in Cali and in the town of Silvia, too.

When my father brought me to Silvia the first time, he didn't do anything to hint at the significance of that place. We had gone to see the weekly Wednesday market during which all the Guambianos brought their wares to sell and buy. Piles of mangos, stacks of sweet *panela*, tables laden with *plátanos* and yuca. These things were interspersed with handwoven blankets and the ponchos the Indians wore, the scarves and hats, the *mochilas* in bright stripes.

After visiting the market, rich in exotic smells and a cacophony of sounds, Renzo had driven me into the reservation to the house of an old friend, a Guambiano named Felipe. "He's a sort of healer," my father had told me. When we arrived at his little two-room house in the mountains, Felipe motioned for me to sit on the bed, the only real piece of furniture in the dirt-floored room. A television set with wonky antennae was across from the bed, a thick wool blanket pulled taut over the mattress. When I sat down, he offered me coffee, but my father discreetly shook his head.

"You don't want to drink the water here," my father whispered to me in English. My mother had told me about a time she had visited a poor family and the woman had offered pineapple juice. My mother had accepted this generous offering from a woman who had almost nothing. She knew the juice mixed with water would make her sick, but she drank it anyway.

Felipe wore the traditional dress of the Guambianos (a man's blue wool skirt, lace-up boots, and a black bowler hat), and when he smiled at me, his missing teeth and scores of wrinkles popped out like trophies of his life.

"He remembers your mom," my father had translated for me when Felipe said something that, between his accented Spanish and gaps in his teeth, I couldn't understand.

Now I wonder if he also remembered Beth, if he had seen my father with this other woman.

Felipe pointed to my face, then my belly.

"He remembers when Nance was pregnant with you."

Although we had declined coffee, Felipe returned from the other room of the house with his own cup of coffee and trailed by a tiny child. Ceci later told me that Felipe was gay and had adopted the children that surrounded him like grandchildren. The little sprite was the size of a two year old, although she must have been older because she was holding a coffee cup in her hands. She wore a hand-embroidered dress and a little pink and blue crocheted hat. The coffee in the cup was milky, probably sweetened with *panela,* a sugar cane sweetener that was sold in brown bricks at the market in Silvia. Watching her, I wondered about the warnings I had heard as a child, that coffee stunts the growth of small children. When I was her age, I had not been drinking coffee; I had been wetting the bed and crying for my mother. I thought of Gabriel García Márquez's character Aureliano Buendía, who before facing a firing squad requests coffee as his dying wish. Coffee, the drink of martyrs and leaders, strong men and fearless women. And, apparently, diminutive children.

Felipe said something more and laughed a gap-toothed and joyous laugh.

"He says you look just like her," my father translated.

One Hundred Years of Solitude was published just before my mother first arrived in Colombia, when magical realism was part of the landscape, not a literary genre. When healers and lost daughters, secret affairs and illegitimate children were the rule, not the exception. Before literature stole away rainstorms of fireflies and sleeping sicknesses, these things existed in Colombia and were not flights of fancy.

And now I wasn't sure if this brother four months my junior was any more real than the Guambiano himself. Gabriel García Márquez says that an experience only needs to feel real in order for it to be so. But the memory of a little girl's sweetened coffee and these email exchanges that could be wiped away at the press of a button felt as unreal as any fairy tale or fiction. I didn't know how to believe in these things that felt conjured from imagination.

16

WHEN MY HALF BROTHER CALLED AGAIN, I agreed to meet him. How could I refuse him? And the itch of curiosity had become an infection that spread into my nerves and brain cells and blood— the very blood that I shared with this stranger. I needed to meet him.

"I'm going to bring my husband," I warned him. I wouldn't be going anywhere without Dave. I would need him to prop me up.

Despite the Colombian connection and the broad range of bars and restaurants in the Bay Area, we agreed to meet at a spot on the 101, a Mexican American joint that served taco salads and fried ice cream, a choice as randomly absurd as eating at a crepes restaurant my first night in Colombia.

El Torito's yellow marquee was easy to spot from the freeway. As Dave took the exit, I let the movement of the cloverleaf jerk me from left to right as if I were nothing more than a puppet or a rag doll. Inside, the dining room was filled with families eating their weeknight dinners, but Dave and I headed toward the bar, where flat boleros alternated with Top 40 and advertisements for strawberry margaritas made me nauseous. We ordered drinks, whatever was on tap.

The beers sweated in their thick glasses. The bartender wiped down the bar. Somewhere a child shrieked, but I couldn't tell if it was in laughter or tears. A young man in baggy shorts and a T-shirt walked in.

"Is that him?" I whispered to Dave.

Dave looked at this man who had a trim black beard, thick ponytail, almond eyes. He looked back at me. "You think?"

In Spanish, the verb *conocer* means both to meet and to get to know. When I first went to Colombia, Renzo and his wife had seemed desperate for me to conocer the country, to see everything and do everything as if they could make up a lifetime in a single month. Once I rode along with Ceci in the Suzuki as she ran errands: the market, her sister's house. We stopped at a street-side stand to buy a Styrofoam cup of *arroz con leche*. As I took small bites of the rice pudding—a little dull to my overstimulated American palate—Ceci unfolded the bills she had received as change for her purchase. She stopped and held one up to the afternoon sun.

"Es falso," she had said. She showed it to me, but all Colombian currency looked fake to me. Without knowing what the original looked like, there was no way for me to recognize something false.

At the next stop, Ceci bought a doohickey of some kind at the mechanic, something mysterious for the Suzuki. I waited in the passenger seat, and when she returned she slammed her door shut, turned the ignition, and spun out of the parking lot.

"Vámonos," she had said, a sneaky smile on her face. "I gave them the counterfeit money."

And just like that, the difference between real and fake blurred. I could see that if we agreed to believe, perhaps we could make it so.

The man in the beard and shorts approached our table. His resemblance to my father was momentarily paralyzing: the same eyes, the shape of the face. His beard even echoed that of my father's in the faded black and white photographs, the ones in the box under my bed. It was like seeing a ghost.

We greeted awkwardly, stiff arms and hunched shoulders. How do you greet a ghost? Should we hug or shake hands? Do nothing? We were simultaneously strangers and family, both intimately connected and yet separated by what seemed then to be an impossible distance. Dave and I picked up our pint glasses, and the three of us moved to a booth, where the man ordered a Corona. Even from across the table, the smell of cigarette smoke wafted toward me, and the smell reminded me even more of my father.

"Hello," we said.

"Renzo," I said, trying out the name, my father's name given to a stranger. I watched him as he squeezed lime into the narrow neck of the beer bottle. I wondered if his name felt like an article of clothing he wore awkwardly, if he felt as fake as I did.

"I had a dream about you," I said. The night before I had had a dream about meeting this unknown brother. I dreamed that, even though his name was Renzo, he was called Bob or Jerry. In the dream, I had been so relieved not to have to call this stranger by my father's name. "Can I call you Jerry?" I asked after telling him about the dream.

"Actually, my family calls me Silas."

It was a nickname from his middle name, Silvanus, he explained, chosen by his mother. Maybe she couldn't bear to call him Renzo either. Silvanus was chosen to honor the town of Silvia, where he was conceived four months after I was. I thought of the town with its steep roads and Guambianos. I hadn't noticed anything particularly romantic in Silvia, but maybe, I was beginning to think, I hadn't looked close enough.

There is a dissatisfying kind of relief when you recognize that not only is the thing you feared nonexistent but also that there was never anything to fear to begin with. The first morning I woke up in my father's house in Popayán, I thought of a conversation I had with my mother when I was eight or nine.

"In Colombia, you really have to be vigilant," my mother had said. We must have been doing dishes at the time, an activity we did for many hours, not having a dishwasher for most of my childhood. "The cockroaches come out at night. They can find any bit of leftover grease."

My mother usually washed, and I dried, putting the spoons and forks and knives away in their own neat compartments in the silverware drawer. "They could be all over the kitchen, and then when you turned the light on, they would all disappear. I remember the little scurrying noises they made."

My mother made a face, and I stopped drying to watch her. I couldn't imagine. I couldn't imagine Colombia or her there. "Doña Rosa had a maid who didn't use hot water to wash dishes," my mother said about her former mother-in-law. "I always washed dishes with hot water, even if I had to heat it on the stove. That's the only way to keep cockroaches at bay. Sometimes," she said as if I wasn't already scared enough, "we would wake up and find cockroaches in our shoes."

From the safety of the sheets and blankets of the bed in my father's house, I had leaned over the edge of the bed to scan the floor, where pools of Andean sunlight fell. The whole room had a yellow glow from the sun and the turmeric-colored walls of the bedroom, which my father had said was mine. My own bedroom in his house. Or, I see now, a child's bedroom—any child. I peered into my shoe as the canaries cackled from the courtyard.

No cockroaches.

This was what it was like to meet Silas for the first time.

After avoiding his calls and insisting I wasn't ready to meet him, I found that he was simply a person, a young man my own age, both a stranger and also something else. And so we agreed to meet again, this time just the two of us. I would encounter my brother without the security of my husband.

Walking toward the pizzeria, I twisted my wedding ring on my finger. My footsteps on the sidewalk sounded like the clatter of cowboys' spurs. He was already there when I pushed open the heavy door, and we were shown to a table with a checkered cloth.

"Renzo said you and your mom didn't want to meet us," he told me after we had ordered beer and pizza—cheese and sausage and green peppers to share. He had begun to unspool the story, our story, and each rotation got more knotted.

"But we never knew about you," I cried. "My mom didn't either." I didn't tell him about "Love the One You're With"; I wasn't sure yet if he was a Stephen Stills kind of person. I didn't know anything about him.

"We searched for you, but we didn't know you had Renzo's last name."

I had been given my father's last name; my half brother had his first name. Proof, I suppose, of my legitimacy and his legacy. Our mothers, independently of each other, had kept a tie, a daily reminder of the man they had each loved or needed or both.

"My mom was married to a Colombian man she met in college," he told me. "At Carleton College."

"The Minnesota connection," I said. "Carleton."

"Right. They got married and moved to Colombia and then got divorced."

The waitress placed a large pizza on a little stand in the middle of the table. "You two need anything else?" she asked in a way that made me think she thought we were a couple. How strange, I thought, to have a brother.

"But she stayed in Colombia after the divorce," Silas explained, as cheese stretched between a slice and his plate.

"That's when she met my mom," I said.

"And our dad."

The way he said this, "our dad," was both shocking and strangely comforting. For a child with no siblings, there is no plural possessive when referring to parents. The world is often singular and sometimes lonely. I had a sudden urge to reach across the table and touch his hand, but instead I managed to bump the pizza. Silas caught it just before it toppled off the table.

"Nice one, Sis," he said, and the world and all its complications seemed, just for a split second, to simplify into the familial relationship of brother and sister.

Even when I had stepbrothers, they never called me anything remotely endearing. Despite spending five years sharing the same bathroom and washing dishes together, we remained, stubbornly, strangers. We spoke when we had to, but we were always divided. It was a choice I had made then, but it didn't need to be the one I made now.

"Were you born in Colombia, too?" I asked.

He shook his head. "When my mom got pregnant, she went back

to Arkansas. That's where I was born. She decided that your mom and Renzo had a better chance of making it."

A better chance?

My mother had grown up living alongside not only three brothers but also the comings and goings of exchange students. My grandparents, although they didn't begin to travel until they were older, hosted students from Thailand, Japan, Norway, and Egypt, teaching their children the value of international relations. My mother had studied both French and Spanish in high school and couldn't wait to explore a new country. But when she arrived, she could barely understand the language, finding that textbook Spanish bore little resemblance to reality. And when she tired of the endless meals of beans and rice at the boardinghouse, she would buy mini-wieners from the grocery store and eat them cold, right out of the can, desperate for familiar flavors and textures. My mother, despite longing for the excitement and novelty that was Colombia, could hardly have been expected to square what she had imagined with the reality of life in a foreign country and an artist husband. Despite Beth's optimism, my parents didn't make it.

"Did you see him when you were a kid?" I asked.

"A couple times," he said.

He had met his father. Our father. A couple times. I had to shift the ideas I had in my head of what a child of my father was. To me, my father wasn't really a father, and his not seeing me grow up was proof of that. My understanding that he had never been a father to anyone had served, in my mind, to almost absolve him. His lack of contact, his obtuse letters, his distance had somehow been forgivable because he was so distant. But now to hear that he had met his son, which meant that he had in some way been a father to him, confused me with a sort of jealousy that wasn't envious.

"We lived in Connecticut for a while, and he was there once."

"I never met him until I went to Colombia in college," I said, trying to keep the bitterness from my voice. Trying to keep it from my heart, too, I suppose.

"We looked for you, you know," Silas said. He picked up his pint of beer. "My mom and I tried to find you."

I tried to picture what that search would have looked like ten, fifteen years earlier. Before the internet, before email, before I knew anything about Colombia. How would the two of them have gone about searching for a half sister? Did they hire a private detective? Did they comb municipal records in public libraries? Did they simply call around to friends and acquaintances?

Before I could ask, Silas said, "My mom knew your mom's last name, so we looked for you."

I nodded. Of course they could never have found us that way. My mother kept my last name until she got married a second time, both of us struggling through Minnesota in the 1980s with that Spanish surname, with the *j* that sounds like an *h*. When my mother got divorced the second time, she returned to her maiden name, having found that changing names with each marriage did something to one's identity. I certainly hadn't been interested in taking my husband's last name. It had nothing to do with feminism or women's liberation. It had everything to do with identity and ownership. I would forever have a name that linked me with not only the legacy of my ancestors but also my own being. Kindergarten school pictures, summer camp nametags, graduation certificates, piano recital programs on yellow paper.

17

A FEW WEEKS LATER WHEN WE MET AGAIN, I told Silas about the photograph of the boy under the glass on the desk in my father's studio. The white borders, the gray background, the wide-set eyes of the boy, his oval face.

"He told me that the person in the picture was the son of an old girlfriend," I said to this man who looked so much like my father. His eyes were so brown they were almost black. He had a crooked tooth in front, one next to the incisor that overlapped the next one as if trying to get a better view, fighting for attention. We were drinking beers at our apartment, and I watched him take a sip of beer, the smell of Corona mixing with my memories of Club Colombia beer, making me feel confused and somehow lightheaded. I took a sip of my own beer. "Which I guess was true," I said.

Silas nodded again. He nodded, not in agreement, but in that California way of recognition, confirmation, perhaps an affirmation he wished he could have. "When I was a kid, he kept saying he would buy me a ticket to visit him. But he never did. Fuck. I was eight years old thinking I was really going to get to know my dad and go to Colombia and then nothing. I got so fucking sick of waiting for him."

I didn't care if it had been the 1970s. I didn't care if the players in this farce had been hippies. A brother and a sister and so many secrets. We were children, the responsibility—the duty, the privilege, the obligation—of this person who had lied to us.

"That's why I stopped contacting him. I was done with him. That shit. In high school . . ." Silas trailed off. "I did some crazy shit. And I just couldn't take it anymore."

In high school, I thought, was when I had reached out. My teenage rebellion had taken the form of writing letters to connect with this father, not to cut him out. Like a revolving door, our father had lost one child only to gain another.

I can't help picturing that moment. Perhaps Renzo had just gone to the post office where he kept a box, number 672. He used a little key to open the metal box only to find—could it have been?—two envelopes sent from the United States. They were both dirty, and one might have been torn in one corner, victim of the unreliable mail delivery system in Colombia, where letters were occasionally intercepted and sometimes never made it to their final destinations. Renzo would have seen one envelope with the familiar round letters of his son. And the other would have been a new script, small and tentative. But the return address in Minnesota would have made his heart catch in his throat. Maybe he brought both letters to a café, where he ordered a *tinto* (a strong black coffee served in a little white cup) and took several sips of scalding liquid before tearing open the envelopes. Perhaps he let the letters sit on the table for a few minutes, long enough to have a friend stop by and clap him on the back, maybe a student who called him "Don Renzo." Maybe an attractive woman around his age (a woman I would later meet on a plane to Popayán) watched his reaction as he read Silas's letter filled with sorrow and disgust. Maybe Silas wrote that he would never write again, maybe he wrote that he hated him. And then, maybe Renzo opened the other letter, my school picture falling from between the pages to the concrete floor of the café. Renzo would have bent down to pick up the picture and stare at it before opening the letter. Reeling from his son's dismissal, he might have had tears in his eyes, his vision blurry, and when he first looked at my tenth-grade school picture he might have thought he was looking at my mother, his ex-wife, in a time warp of emotions. And maybe that confluence of correspondences made everything that happened after possible. From the lies to the truths, from the sorrow to the anger.

"Recently I started thinking about you again," Silas said. "I mean, screw him, but I have a sister."

■ ■ ■

There was a word to ponder. *Sister.* There is an entire pseudoscience around birth order, pop psychology that aligns one's place in the family with characteristics and outlooks and behavior. "Only child" is its own side note, usually, those of such unusual parents, selfish and probably entitled parents who chose to bring only one child into the world, repopulation be damned. I suppose if I had grown up under China's one-child policy, my status as only child would have felt normal. But in the United States—not even just the United States but most of Western societies, most societies in general—multiple children are expected. Brothers, sisters. These turn into uncles and aunts when nieces and nephews come along. Siblings that share the burden of farming or the family business, the care of the elderly, and the maintenance of the estate. I read about the sisters in *Little Women* and *Pride and Prejudice.* Only children were the anomaly. Maybe that's why I was drawn to Anne Shirley and Rebecca of Sunnybrook Farm. Of course, these characters not only had no siblings—they generally had no parents either. It had always seemed to me that lacking siblings was correlated with orphanhood. Perhaps I was half an orphan: mother only, no father.

Sister. I was a sister. It dawned on me that I had been a sister my whole life without knowing it. All the times I said I was an only child had been a lie. Through my father's lie, I became a liar. And my life suddenly felt like a lie, too. There was what didn't happen, what could have happened, and what did.

I was lied to by my father. I wasn't an only child. I was a sister. I had always been a sister. The anger that I had seen in Silas surfaced in me, taking hold of my insides with bony fingers that tugged toward resentment.

In the English translation of Gabriel García Márquez's *One Hundred Years of Solitude,* the Buendía family tree is included in the front of the book. It maps the parents and lovers, the wives and children, the bastards and angels. In strong black lines it connects each person, one to the next in clearly demarcated logic. My father told me that in the original Spanish (if he is to be believed) no genealogical history is included. García Márquez never sketched one out, never planned for such a rudimentary explanation to be part of his book. Families do what trees do: they grow and change and modify themselves to fit.

The lemon tree in my father's back courtyard had a branch that rested on a makeshift support as it grew heavy with lemons. A plastic footstool or ladder kept the branch from breaking off and falling to the ground. And the tree was still beautiful, still bore fruit, which Ceci squeezed and made into lemon mousse for New Year's Eve.

New Year's Eve in Colombia is a much bigger celebration than Christmas. There are parties and rituals. One must wear yellow (usually in the form of polyester underwear sold on every corner at the end of December) and carry lentils. If you want to travel during the coming year, you must walk a suitcase around the block. For good fortune, you might create an *año nuevo muñeco,* an effigy of the old year, a figurine to be set on fire, removed from memory with a strike of a match. The carefully constructed life-size dolls wear old hats and trousers, some wear T-shirts and work boots. Before the practice was banned, at midnight these *muñecos* were burned, letting last year's disappointments and tragedies disperse in clouds of ash, making room for this year's promises.

When the music swirled during my New Year's Eve in Colombia, I recognized that this was what my life could have been. I might have been one of the small children dodging between uncles and grandmothers, running with brothers and sisters. At the time, it was all complete fantasy—conjecture based on wishing and wondering. Now I saw that this story had another element. A brother and a sister sneaking *dulces* and *caramelos* from the table of food, leading younger cousins in hijinks and setting off firecrackers.

18

WHEN DAVE PULLED UP at the address Silas had given us, the first thing he noticed was the wide gold Buick Skylark parked in the driveway.

"Look at the car," he said, "from the sixties, maybe seventies."

On the other side of the Skylark was another car under a tarp. Dave lifted the canvas. "Another beaut," he said. "A convertible."

When Silas answered the door, Dave nodded toward the driveway. "Nice car," he said, communicating in that way men do, speaking a language more complex to me than Spanish.

Silas nodded back. "My '69 Cutlass."

Dave, after recently inheriting money from his great-aunt, had bought a Mazda convertible. First we had looked at used Honda del Sols and then had test-driven several Miatas. These little two-seaters were for sale by owners whose wives were having babies. I could see the pity in Dave's face when the men caressed the hoods and explained why they were selling.

"Your life is over when you have kids," Dave had said after buying a mint-condition 1990 Miata. He's more than six feet tall and had removed some of the stuffing from the driver's seat in order to fit inside. He was better at adjusting to life than I was.

We followed Silas into his house, a cozy rental that smelled vaguely of marijuana and stale beer.

"This is my mom, Beth."

At an oak dining-room table sat a woman with grayish-blonde hair and blue eyes. "I remember your mom," Beth said in greeting. She was older than I expected, a little disappointing in her ordinariness. "Does she still live in Minnesota?"

I nodded. She nodded back.

She wasn't a seductress or vixen. I had hoped that she would provide some clue to events that led to this half brother. But she seemed nice and was unremarkable in appearance. She was closer in age to my father than my mother, and she had only recently gotten married again. She worked in a food co-op, liked to do tile mosaics. My own mother had dabbled in both painting and textiles. I remembered the comforting thud of the treadle against the warp as she formed lines and circles, curves and shapes out of wool and cotton in shades of browns and oranges. The weavings (the ones that she completed, anyway) eventually hung on the walls of our apartment until she got remarried and they were folded into fourths and stored in cardboard boxes. Beth's art, in contrast, was solid and bold. Silas pointed out a couple of pieces of her artwork that decorated his living room. Tiny squares of vibrant color came together to form a flower, a dolphin, a face, hung beside a sketch in ink that could have been made only by our father.

Beth's husband came in from the backyard and introduced himself. By some strange coincidence, his elderly father lived in Minnesota next door to my great-aunt in their retirement community. Beth only nodded again. Like Ceci, she seemed to find nothing odd in this familial situation, perhaps willing to take family where she could get it.

"Anika," I heard Silas call from outside. I went through the kitchen to find him standing in front of the grill with a young man.

"This is my brother," Silas said, tongs in one hand.

Silas's brother was blond like their mother. Where it wasn't a ruddy red, his skin was pale, almost literally white. He looked nothing like Silas, although I wasn't sure if I did either. Before this meeting, I had studied my face in the bathroom mirror while Dave was at work. What Silas had inherited from Renzo was much more obvious: the black curly hair, the dark eyes, the thin chicken legs. I am much more my mother's daughter, with a wide gummy smile and thick thighs. But my coloring, considered dark by Minnesota standards, clearly comes from my father, as if he, the artist, was the one who got to choose the shade of skin, the color of the eyes.

I didn't embrace my Latino heritage until I left for college, when I left behind my white mother and my white friends and my white relatives. I joined the Hispanic Student Association and listened to Spanish-language rock and roll and ate Mexican *buñuelos* and *arroz con pollo*. We went to movies and met in the library for study sessions. We held bake sales and salsa dances. It was 1994, and Cesar Chavez had just died, his death still inspiring marginalized Latinos and farmworkers. We lobbied the administration to allow us to change our name— radically—to the *Latino* Student Association. *Hispanic* implies a language, a common Spanish origin, and *Hispanic* is an English word, given—not taken. And not all Latinos are Hispanic. We don't all grow up speaking Spanish, we're not all descended from Spaniards. The U.S. Census uses *Hispanic* and *Latino* interchangeably as if words hold no meaning. Origin, country of birth, heritage. It's all lumped together. "Too political," the college administration said.

How differently we hear the sounds of words.

Even after I learned how to dance the merengue, my Mexican American friends would good-naturedly call me "half-breed."

Me with my white mother and Latino father. Me with a half brother.

Looking at him manning the grill, I saw that we both have something of the same half-and-half look to us. Not quite foreign, not quite domestic. We could be Italian, Middle Eastern, French, American Indian.

Children get half their DNA from their mothers and half from their fathers (although there is a little fuzzy math there in that you get just a bit more from your mother on account of her X chromosome), and siblings share half their DNA. Half siblings, although they also get half their DNA from the same parent, share only an average of 25 percent of their DNA, similar to a first cousin. And yet I already felt more connected to my new half brother than to my father, with whom I share as much DNA as I do with my mother. Silas and I were nothing alike and at the same time similar beyond measure.

I shook hands with Silas's brother. We accepted beers and plates of food, and all of us sat at the patio table together.

"My half brother has a half brother," I joked.

Then Silas's brother said, "I have another half brother, too."

We are all half something, I supposed. Half our mothers and half our fathers. Half our upbringing and half our genes. Half our fantasies, half our realities. And after all the halves come the quarters, the eighths, until we can't be divided anymore, the pieces of ourselves too small to count. I rearranged the punch line: my half brother has a half brother who has a half brother.

19

SILAS BEGAN CALLING ME, phoning to chat as if we were friends, leaving messages that began "Hey, Sis," as if we were siblings. And when I returned the voice mail, I would say, "This is your sister," just to try out the words, to experiment with the way they felt in my mouth and in my heart.

When we met for lunch or went out for a drink, we didn't talk about what might have been. But I couldn't help imagining a life I had never lived. Imagine if there had been no secrets, if my half brother and I had grown up knowing about one another, if there had been weekends spent together, phone calls, Christmas cards. We might have gone to Colombia together that first time in 1995, both of us twenty-one years old, both of us unsure of what lay ahead. Both of us together.

We might have met at the Miami airport, Silas flying from San Francisco, me from Minneapolis. We might have sat together in the exit row of flight 965, and when the man across the seat asked us if we were visiting family, we would have said yes without hesitation. We would have ordered beers from the flight attendant instead of cloying Coca-Colas, and the two of us would have gotten punchy during the flight, hiding our nerves and insecurities with jokes and alcohol. We would have exited the plane together, handing over passports with—albeit different last names—the same almond eyes. We would have disembarked and stepped through the automatic doors into the Macondo-like night, and Renzo would have seen both his children together, side by side for the first time. And he would have wept with his own what-could-have-beens.

Instead, we were just getting to know each other.

"You have a brother, so you don't understand how weird this is," I accused him.

"I've never had a sister," he countered.

I could only nod and agree: it was weird no matter how you looked at it.

Once when Silas and I met for lunch near his office, he told me about working as something of a corporate spy, going to competitors, finding out secrets.

I pumped him for information. "You just walk in there?" I asked.

He took a bite of Thai chicken and nodded. Silicon Valley tech companies were desperate to beat each other to the market, to look into crystal balls to see the IPOs and buyouts. While I was working on a master's degree, my half brother had barely graduated from high school. But he had worked his way up from floor sweeper to something even more integral to his company.

"You just pretend? Like you work there?"

"You'd be amazed at how little people pay attention," he said. "If you act like you belong, no one notices."

In the late 1960s or early 1970s, my father had been suspected of being a spy. I don't know for sure whether he was or wasn't. My mother insists he was too disorganized to be a spy, but I do know he worked for the U.S. State Department. And someone considered him interesting enough to investigate crudely. My father arrived home to my parents' apartment one evening to find the rooms ransacked, the drawers turned upside down, the closets rifled through. It was one of a string of apartments and houses my parents rented during their marriage, from a duplex in Minneapolis to a flat above a noisy discotheque in Popayán to a place in the capital city that came with a maid (paid for by his parents). I wish I could step into the shoes of the intruders and look through the objects that had made up my parents' lives. I picture tubes of paint and ink-stained tables, half-loomed weavings, and brown rings left behind from cups of coffee. I imagine there was perhaps an unmade bed with sheets tangled from early-morning lovemaking and cotton T-shirts hanging in the bathroom, turned stiff after drying. I picture pans with glued-on rice soaking in the makeshift kitchen, leaving a chore that might have filled my mother with rage.

Growing up, I remember outbursts. At times they were unfounded, but my mother's anger bubbled and spilled, occasionally heated by some source or another. Once she broke a pitcher of orange juice on the kitchen floor before work, and her anger had shattered, scattered as far as the shards of glass. Another time, I refused to come inside at bedtime, and I remember her fury as she dragged me indoors in the waning light of summer sunset. Postpartum, my mother had been depressed, my father said. But she was responsible for a helpless baby, stuck in the house in Popayán. Her body and its fluctuating hormones perhaps turned her anxieties to anger, especially when my father returned home late at night.

But I don't know. Maybe the anger started earlier. When my mother's water broke, she was brought to the Popayán municipal hospital to be cared for by a friend of my father's, a doctor who had never delivered a baby before. And while my mother labored and swore, pushed and shouted, my father and his friend drank *tragos* of whiskey.

Or even before that, when she and my father would yell at one another so that the widow on the other side of the wall could hear their arguments. I can imagine that my mother's anger would start deep in her chest and work its way out to her fingertips, forcing her hands into fists, contorting her face. I know that feeling because that's how my anger felt. As a child I was taught to tear paper bags as an alternative to throwing my toys. But nothing releases anger better than destroying something you love.

Whatever reason the ransackers had for searching my parents' apartment in Colombia, the invasion was never repeated. My parents moved to Bogotá shortly after the break-in. It didn't occur to me until much later to wonder what was found and what they were looking for.

I told Silas about the spy suspicions, but he only shrugged. "Could be."

I wondered if perhaps he was done wondering about our dad.

I certainly wasn't.

20

WHEN I HAD VISITED MY FATHER YEARS EARLIER, his need to show me everything in Colombia had been an urgent, palpable thing that followed us everywhere. I know he needed to show me Colombia so that I would love it as much as he did. But I think he also wanted to form memories with me, to create something between us that hadn't existed. We needed to go to the village of Silvia because he had never read me bedtime stories. He needed to give me a tour of his studio because I had never been to his art shows. He needed to take me to a movie because we had never watched cartoons together on Saturday mornings.

My brother and I, too, needed to do activities together, to form memories. It felt, at times, a little manufactured and artificial, but perhaps all of life is simply manufactured moments strung together.

When my mother came to visit the summer I met my brother, I offered to introduce her to Silas. "I'd love to meet him," she said. "And I'd love to see Beth, too."

That I wasn't ready for, but when she came to California, I arranged a dinner with my mother and my new half brother. Dave and I grilled kabobs and made couscous, one of the few meals we knew how to make. I marinated the beef and skewered the vegetables while we waited for Silas to arrive.

When he walked into the apartment, my mother flushed and floundered and then said, "Nice to meet you." And they stood in the doorway with their arms at their sides.

Silas was nearly the same age our father had been when my mother first met the Colombian artist with the beard and black eyes.

Silas's ponytail mitigated the déjà vu somewhat, but he had the same slight build, the same brown arms. Of course, my father had worn the uniform of a hippie (beads and bell-bottoms), while Silas was a California kid, raised on the streets of San Francisco's Mission District and Redwood City's Mexican neighborhoods. His jeans were baggy, and he wore Vans, his black T-shirt advertising something none of us knew anything about. I could tell that my mother was eyeing him all throughout the dinner around our little kitchen table, perhaps thinking of the old black and white photos of her husband with the mustache and the sunglasses.

Or maybe she was remembering him in real life, her memories not dependent on old photographs.

"Renzo," she said, meaning my—our—father, "was so handsome."

We all nodded, another moment for our shared memories.

Then, after her visit, another moment. Silas took us to San Francisco, where he had grown up. He maneuvered through San Francisco's Friday evening traffic as haphazardly as Ceci driving the Suzuki around motorbikes and cattle in Popayán. We would see a band, stop by a couple bars, check out a club where his brother was doing sound, maybe get something to eat. With Dave in the back leaning between the seats, and Silas at the wheel, I felt a strange sort of symmetry between this moment and all those rides in the Andes.

"This is where I used to walk my little brother home from school every day," Silas told us after he parked and we emerged into the cold night air of the Mission District.

I pictured a dark-haired boy watching a little blond one, navigating the sidewalks and red lights. My own childhood walks home from school were unaccompanied except for the imaginary companions I invented. Sometimes there were orphans and others pioneer girls, all the characters I saw in my mind's eye inspired by the books I had been exposed to. In each one I was the protagonist, the star, the heroine of the story. Maybe that's what happens when you're an only child and have no other children to startle you back to reality—you begin to believe that you are the center, the most important. And I'm not sure that's selfishness. It isn't that an only child feels entitled or that she must get her own way. It's that there is no other way, everything experienced solo.

"Tacos?" Silas asked as we walked by a storefront.

Dave and I followed him into the *taquería,* where a woman in a white apron and white cap smiled at us.

"A la órden," she said as we entered. She was round and brown, her black hair pulled back tight under the cap, and I could tell she assumed we were people who spoke Spanish. But despite my brother's black hair and Colombian blood, he didn't speak much Spanish, and neither did Dave. So I ordered the *taquitos* and *bocadillos* as if I spoke this language every day.

We had just unwrapped our food at a white Formica table when the glass door swung wide and a guy stumbled in. He was like a frat boy from central casting—ball cap backward, shaggy blond-brown hair, stocky build.

"Hey, man," the guy said, approaching our table.

We were the only customers in the shop. I glanced over to the counter, but the woman had disappeared. Dave and I hesitated while Silas looked up, his hands still wrapped around his taco.

"Can you spare some money for the BART? I need some train fare to get back to the East Bay," the guy said.

I watched Silas eye him up and down with a look of disgust.

"I just got jumped by some spics."

Spics. A word I hadn't heard until a college friend—one of those Latinos who had grown up with a mamá who administered Vick's Vapo-Rub and recited rosaries—threw it around.

"Get a bunch of spics together," she had said while we were cased by a security guard at the mall, "and you'll get followed around."

My white maternal family marveled at my tan skin, and classmates in my suburban school touched my smooth dark-brown hair. It wasn't until I was forced to fill in the demographic information on the

Pre SAT that I realized there was a designation for everyone. After shading in the little circles that corresponded to the letters and numbers of my name, birth date, and address, a question I'd never answered before stopped me. *Race.*

It was 1990, and these categories were, for me at age fifteen, new. *Black*? Not me and not any of the other students in this suburban classroom. *Asian*? Nope, although several of my friends would fill in that bubble. *White (Not Hispanic)*? Yes—wait. I looked at it again and then glanced around the room. No one else's eyes were wandering. No one else seemed confused by the options. I was white, wasn't I? That was the circle most of my friends would shade. My mother, my maternal grandparents, all my Minnesota relatives for generations. I moved my pencil, and the point hovered above the circle.

But what about *Not Hispanic*? I scanned down the list and found *Hispanic*. It said "of Mexican or South American heritage." Was that me? I was born in Colombia, as I would tell anyone. I had undeniable South American heritage. But could that be me?

Most people are born into families who look like them with the family structure in place. Brothers, sisters, parents. Children adopted into families of different ethnic backgrounds must, at some point, have the realization that they are different from their parents, but I suspect that the realization of being different doesn't usually come in a rush, is already known if not understood. Of course, the realization of being a sibling also isn't something that usually has to be told.

Yet for me, that awareness seemed to happen over and over again. I would forget that I was different until suddenly someone would remind me. I was a freshman in college when Dr. Waters, an English professor obsessed with Milton and Chaucer, had offered to let me take the ESL version of the basic skills test.

"ESL?" I had asked him, confused. I was standing in front of his lectern as he packed up his papers and books. He was a small craggy man with a face so wrinkled it looked like his eyeballs would be sucked into his skull.

"English as a Second Language," he enunciated. This was the same man who had read my essays all semester and scratched As across the top of the dot matrix printouts. This is the man who called on me in class as I (with unaccented English) responded to questions of comprehension and theme. "There's a special test for people like you," he said. "Hispanics take it."

But I had never had the word *spic* spat at me. I was unprepared, then, for my brother's reaction to the guy in the *taquería.*

"Some what?" Silas asked, not looking up from his taco.

"Some spics, man," the guy insisted, coming closer to us. His eyes were slightly red, the backward cap a little crooked. Dave and I were silent. "I just need money for the train."

"We got nothing for you." Silas squinted his black eyes and stood up, his chair scraping against the cement floor with a teeth-rattling screech. His shoulders back, chin up, he looked taller and broader than he really was.

The guy swayed a moment and then stumbled back out into the night.

"That prick's never making it out of the Mission," Silas said, sitting back down and picking up his taco again.

And then the three of us began to laugh. We laughed with fear, with relief, with the knowledge that we were in this whole crazy world together. But our laughter was tinged with sadness. My half brother and I were twenty-six years old, and we were laughing together for the first time. And I couldn't help feeling like I had been cheated. By the world. And by my father.

21

I HAD KNOWN MY BROTHER for less than six months when a photograph on my computer one warm sunny day in September showed black, billowy smoke engulfing tall buildings. Looking more closely at the pixilated image on my monitor, I recognized that it was the World Trade Center, and I read the headline and wondered what kind of joke this was. And for the first time since returning from Colombia, I had a sense of danger everywhere.

On September 12, the first lists of victims appeared in the newspaper. I cut out the names as though by saving the newsprint I could save them. These people had existed, had had fathers and mothers and brothers and sisters. The next day more names appeared, and it was clear there would be too many to count. I took an old plastic water bottle and stuffed the newspaper inside like a pointless message. Dave and I drove to Santa Cruz, where I flung the bottle into the water from a rocky cliff above the Pacific Ocean. I couldn't see them, but I had heard that the Coast Guard and military ships were patrolling the coastlines. I thought of Colombia, which, like the United States, borders two oceans, her shores as vulnerable as ours. I held hands with Dave as we watched the bottle bobbing up and down in an eddy of churning water going nowhere.

Even though we had known each other only a few months, Silas and I arranged to meet at a candlelight vigil that was being organized at San Jose State University, where I was in graduate school. On Friday we stood on the campus, holding candles protected by paper cups. The scent of eucalyptus from the trees that dotted the quad reminded me of Colombia and made me feel out of place, magnified a sense of homesickness that the tragedy had brought on. If I had visited Colombia after moving to California, these trees wouldn't have smelled so foreign. If the planes had not crashed into their intended targets, innocent people would not have died. If I had met my brother before all this, he wouldn't have been a stranger.

Later we hung out with a few of Silas's friends at his girlfriend's house. Someone grilled food, which no one ate, and we sipped Coronas on the patio. A kitten who had been abandoned by her mother occupied our attention. People laughed at her miniature pounces and outsized purrs as they told stories about where they were on Tuesday, what they were doing, how their ordinary lives had become just a little less ordinary by being witness to such tragedy. These strangers around me mourned the strangers who had died; we just needed to be with one another, it didn't matter who. Love the one you're with.

I looked over at Silas. My brother. He was mostly silent, didn't say much, absently smoked a cigarette as the kitten attacked his shoelaces. The light from a citronella candle flickered and cast shadows on his face. And the more I watched him, his resemblance to my father faded. He looked less like a ghost or a stranger and more like my brother.

Thousands of people had lost loved ones and family, and yet, in the midst of September 11, I had gained someone. And I was just beginning to realize that I might someday forgive my father for keeping this secret, that maybe I would think about all the choices made and choose to make the most of what had happened. Maybe I could leave behind what hadn't happened and face what had.

That winter, when everyone was still reeling from the events of September 11, still hunkering down in hopes of some kind of self-preservation, Dave's parents came to visit. They were solidly midwestern, even more so than my mother's family. They were churchgoers and socially conservative, he a Vietnam War vet, she a preschool teacher. That was when they were nothing more than a charmingly ordinary Presbyterian couple who had been together nearly since high school. That was before

I noticed any similarities between their marriage and mine. That was before Dave's mom fell ill with a cancer that invaded every part of her.

After 9/11, George W. Bush had urged Americans to spend money and live life as a way to combat the bad guys, and so Dave's parents arrived at our apartment ready to be California tourists despite increased airport security and talk of war, despite his mother's head scarves and a wig with artificial blonde hair. With remnants of chemotherapy still making their way through her body, she was hungry for sensations: touch and smell, sight and taste. We took her to a winery in the Santa Cruz Mountains, and she became giggly and tipsy after a few sips of pinot gris, and to Monterey, where she was sprayed by salty ocean water and teetered on the craggy rocks of the Pacific Coast.

We showed her the spot in Pacific Grove where the monarchs spend the winter. I had first learned about monarchs in elementary school. I learned that the butterflies can't survive the winter in cold places like Minnesota and so fly south. Then, when it's warmer and safer, they fly back again. Year after year monarchs and their descendants find their homes again. In fifth grade I helped my teacher tag the delicate black and orange wings. I carefully brushed off a few scales the way he had taught me and then gently placed a sticker on the spot, a number that would identify that little insect for the next scientist who would find it in a warmer climate.

The monarchs in Pacific Grove come from all over the western United States, looking for their winter homes, the same place their great-grandparents had wintered. They find the spot without the benefit of airmail or email, flying in haphazard zigzags until they make it to the grove of eucalyptus trees. Dave's mom picked her way carefully over the carpet of fallen leaves below the branches on which clung hundreds—maybe thousands—of butterflies. We inhaled the spicy scent of the trees, pointing to the branches where, as a beam of sunlight passed a cluster of what looked like leaves, orange and black wings were suddenly aflutter like the dead rising. Dave's mom stretched her head back to look up, and smiled as the monarchs flitted and swooped and rearranged themselves on their perches. When the sun passed behind a cloud they were still again, awoken only by the warmth of its rays. These monarchs, like the ones I had tagged as a child, had traveled thousands of miles to be in this spot, to spend the winter in a protected grove. They had a homing instinct that drove them and propelled them and gave their lives meaning. Home, their deepest urges called. And they listened.

I understood their instincts; I ached to return to Minnesota. Around us, friends were buying houses and putting down roots, but I wasn't interested in real estate. "When are we going to move back?" I began to ask Dave, knowing it was selfish, knowing I was asking a lot. He had a satisfying career and loved the rocky hikes. I began to worry, though, that something would trap us in San Jose. It seemed that we would get stuck in this arid Mediterranean climate forever, that we might never see scarlet-hued autumn leaves and spring's delicate crabapple blooms again. Minnesota held nothing of the exotic or exciting, but there were my grandparents and, most important, my mother. A single mother and an only daughter. Even though I was no longer technically an only child, I needed my mother again.

"We just met," Silas said when I told him we were planning to move back to Minnesota. I didn't understand then how devastating this news was for him. He had spent his life wondering about his sister only to find her in adulthood—and now to have her ripped away again. It must have been for him an uncomfortable refrain that had been repeated throughout his childhood: the anticipation of family and then the letdown. How could I explain to him that the reality I knew—my Minnesota family, friends, the constancy of winter, spring, summer, fall—tugged at me like an ornery toddler pulling at my sleeve? Although I never doubted the validity of our relationship as brother and sister, it still resided in the realm of what could be, not what was. Putting aside my urge to return to my childhood home required a faith in the future that I couldn't quite muster.

I told him it would be fine. I assured him it wouldn't change anything, even though I knew it would. We barely knew each other, and with distance between us, without the benefit of daily interactions, our tenuous relationship would fall into the same category as mine with my father. Siblings in name only. Now I'm not sure why I was so eager to make that break. But even with a brother, I was an only child, selfish and used to making decisions with only my own needs in mind. Like a petulant homesick camper, I stamped my foot and scowled. I want to go home.

"You can't go yet," my brother insisted.

In 1976, my father must have said, *You can't go.*

I was a toddler crawling on the uneven flagstones of the patio of the haunted house in Popayán, and my mother might have told him, "I want to go to Minnesota."

It would have been a discussion they had had many times. During their nearly six years of marriage, my parents bounced back and forth between Minnesota and Colombia, searching for a place that would make them happy.

"For a visit, fine," my father would have said. "We have to live here in Popayán, though. This is where my work is. You know that."

A few months earlier, my mother had started teaching English to air traffic controllers, young and vibrant men who were learning the language of take-offs and landings, men who were able to guide you to safety. She had befriended one of them, a handsome one. "We should be with my family in Minnesota," she said.

"We tried that. It didn't work. This is where I need to be. To paint." He would have waved his arms, a gesture meant to encompass the haunted house, the baby girl, the mountains, the very air itself.

Before I was born, they lived in Minneapolis, first in the basement of my grandparents' rambler and later in a rented apartment in Uptown. My father had gone to school at the Minneapolis College of Art and Design, and so when our little family arrived in Minneapolis the summer of 1976, they took me to the campus, meandered the nearby art museum. There is a photograph of me with my father sitting at an outdoor café. He holds me in his lap even as I scowl in concentration at something just outside the frame.

"Your parents left you with me," my grandfather told me. "I think they went to a movie," he said, laughing. "You cried your crazy head off. The longest movie ever."

Besides the movie, there was the German restaurant in Minneapolis, where they drank beer on a patio with my grandparents. My father didn't know he was spending his last days with his daughter. And finally, at some point, safe on American soil and having retained a lawyer in secret, my mother gathered her courage and told her husband she wanted a divorce.

"Nance," he must have pleaded, "we can work this out."

"It's no use."

"We'll go to counseling," he tried.

"I want a divorce," she reiterated, as if by saying it over and over he would understand.

"I don't understand," he must have said. Because for this man, infidelity was no reason to dissolve a marriage, estrangement could be cured, and love was worth it. Besides, Beth had already blessed their marriage, had told him they could make it, and he had loved Beth and believed her.

"I don't love you anymore," my mother might have said, although I wonder if that's possible—to say those words to someone you once did.

"I love you and Anika," he said. "Let's make it work."

But her mind was made up. When she had first arrived in Colombia, she had wanted to reinvent herself; now she would do it again. I would never completely understand what it had been like for her. By the time my mother had decided on divorce, she had already imagined her new life, one that did not include a moody artist, one where she was free.

"You can't go," my father must have said.

But she did.

And I would, too.

22

WHEN DAVE AND I ARRIVED IN MINNESOTA to apartment hunt and interview, his mom had just come home under hospice care. She was fifty-two years old but looked ancient, frail, tiny against the white sheets of the hospital bed. Her wisps of hair just starting to grow back looked grayer than her previous blonde. Maybe it was all that absence of color that made her want me to paint her fingernails bright pink. I carefully brushed on the lacquer, one fine stroke at a time, holding her cold hand, the fingers pale with lack of circulation.

My mother-in-law craved sensory stimulation during those final weeks. She cuddled with her husband in their big bed, held hands with her adult sons. She wanted me to massage her palms and knuckles with lavender-scented lotion. Her husband set up a microphone outside the bedroom window to capture the sounds of the early spring birds. The amplified voices filled the sickroom with an extra layer of unfounded optimism.

One night, when we were all eating a makeshift dinner on our laps surrounding what would become her deathbed, a delivery of flowers arrived. It was a vase of yellow roses the color her hair used to be, fair and innocent. She sat up in bed to look at the flowers on the bedside table.

"Bring them closer, Dave," she said.

He stood up and held the heavy vase nearer.

"Closer," she said, and he moved the flowers almost in her lap. She leaned forward and dove her face into the blossoms, closed her eyes, and breathed in deeper.

When I worked in the flower shop in college, I sold centerpieces to disillusioned housewives and single carnations to well-intentioned young men. I stripped the thorns off Colombian-grown roses and gave each stem a fresh cut before wrapping the flowers in butcher paper. Roses could be dangerous; anything that beautiful could hurt you.

"My mother grew yellow roses," Dave's mom said, her voice weak, her nose still in the flowers. "They were in the front yard, by the fence."

I realized suddenly that I knew nothing about her, a woman who had had three sons but loved tea parties and flowers. I touched her hand as my throat closed with the bitter taste of guilt and sorrow. The what-could-have-beens piled around us.

We had to fly back to California, but before our taxi arrived, she pulled one of the yellow roses out of the vase and laid it in Dave's hand. He strapped it to his backpack, and we carried it home with us. The petals were just beginning to curl and dry when Dave's dad called him.

It wasn't fair, I knew, this death of a mother. Dave's mother. He was losing family even as mine seemed to be growing. The intensity of the loss increased the urgency to return to Minnesota, even though she was no longer there. We were young and untethered, free to return home. Going home was what people did, each of us with a homing instinct as strong perhaps as the monarchs'. The following winter, having been hired by a Minnesota company that paid for relocation, we left the eucalyptus trees and the ocean and the half brother. We jammed the Honda hatchback with plants and laundry baskets and headed across the country, the two of us nothing more than instinctual creatures flitting our way home.

A few days before we left, when the movers had already packed our dishes and towels in cardboard boxes, Silas took me to lunch. It was December, but the day was warm and sunny, and I rode in the front seat of the Cutlass convertible. With the top down and the sun shining, the brown vinyl smelled like Colombia with its off-gassing and fine film of pollen dust. As he took the corners, I let myself slide across the slippery seats as off balance as a bottle floating in the ocean waves.

I don't remember where we went, but I remember sitting across a lunch table from Silas, talking without saying anything. He didn't tell me how hurt he was, how abandoned he felt. Instead, he said, "When

I was about eight, Renzo told me he would send me a ticket to go to Colombia. I was so excited."

I didn't find out until later that Silas was the literal dark sheep of the family, that his blond-haired brother had a father who lived with them for several years, a parent he could visit, stay with on weekends, perhaps punctuating Silas's lack of a dad. I had had a grandfather and uncles, a stepfather and stepbrothers, and learned that men will come and go. I didn't make the connection until much later that he was still seeking an ideal of a father figure.

"But he flaked out. I never went."

He was a boy who needed a father, who needed a connection to his Colombian ancestry. And when he finally found it in a sister, she left him.

"You'll have to visit us," I said cheerily. Even though I had always been a pessimist.

"You're really going," he said when we left the restaurant and walked into the white sunlight.

He held open the heavy car door for me, and I nodded. I was sad and so happy at the same time. The sun beat down on our brown heads as we drove down the 101, leaving trails of invisible regrets.

The house we bought in Minneapolis six months later had a small front porch, oak built-ins of the kind you never see in California, the kind that made us repeat how glad we were to be back in Minnesota. The foursquare two-story also had three modest bedrooms, one of which a friend had suggested would make a good nursery. At first we hadn't been sure about having children, then, as we passed thirty, we—especially I—felt the stirrings of a desire so strong it was like a violent undertow pulling me toward motherhood.

There was something about homeownership, too, that made me feel domestic in a way I never had in California. Everything there had felt so impermanent and malleable. During our last month in California, while I was flipping through the pages of some magazine, an earthquake struck. Probably not any worse than a 5.0. We had felt many tiny movements of the earth, but this one was our strongest. Even before I felt it, I heard a whoosh of wood siding and slamming of termite-chewed beams. From my perch on the olive-green futon, I watched the walls swell in and out like some living, breathing creature. The earthquake had lasted less than thirty seconds, but in those moments I could feel the uncertainty of life in this land where the ground literally moved, however minutely, under our feet. Even though the tremor was too small to cause damage, I realized that the apartment building in which we lived was more like a boat floating on a lake than solid construction with deep footings. We were all at the mercy of plate tectonics and the natural world.

Now I craved permanence and even responsibility. In Minnesota, buildings are erected on solid bedrock, limestone and shale, sandstone and dolomite. These buildings don't have to withstand the kind of rocking and swaying that happen in places where the earth is less firm, places where, I was beginning to think, reality itself was less solid.

And in that solid darkness of our quiet bedroom, one night the world shifted again, showed itself again to be less immobile than we thought. Dave rolled over in bed to face me, his features blurry and familiar. "Let's make a baby," he whispered in the glow of Minneapolis streetlights.

And within three months, we had a beginning. Is this how it happens? I wondered. When I had asked Ceci if she wanted to have kids and she told me of her miscarriages, I didn't connect the dots then, didn't consider that she had held grown life—however briefly—within her. Life that would have been evidence of her and my father's union. That's what pregnancy felt like, especially at first, like physical evidence of love, a bit of magic and reality.

Not that I found it all magical.

"What did we do?" I asked Dave those first few weeks. "What the fuck did we do?"

But as soon as we had our first ultrasounds, I took my mother out to lunch and pulled the sonogram picture from my purse.

"I have news."

Even as I pushed the black and white image across the table, she was already in tears.

"I was starting to think you two would never have a baby," she said.

Me too, I thought.

And six weeks later, on Easter Sunday, I called Renzo. My father. To tell my other parent I was going to be a parent.

It wasn't, I told myself, that I had forgiven him. It wasn't, I was certain, that all my anger had dissipated. But there was something about the beginning of a life that puts other things in perspective.

"My dear Anika," he said, the delay between each sentence an echo that bounced our words around.

"Guess what?" I said before he could broach any topic, before he could ask me how I felt or what I was thinking. I didn't want to talk about his secrets and lies. I wanted to tell him my own news. "We're having a baby," I said. "I'm pregnant."

My father began to laugh and said, "Wow." He laughed, and I assumed it was from joy.

"Wow, I'm so happy for you, my dear," he said.

And despite the remnants of my anger, I felt proud, like I had done something amazing. I thought of that time I had played Poohsticks with Ceci and María Fernanda and how proud I had felt of my little stick, even though I had nothing to do with its progress.

23

THE FIRST TIME the ob-gyn squirted gel on my abdomen and ran the fetal Doppler over the slight rise in my belly, a frantic pounding suddenly filled the exam room. It was quick like a butterfly caught in a jar flapping uselessly to escape. The sound coming through the speakers of the machine pulsated in the tiny room.

"That's the heartbeat," the doctor said, smiling.

When my mother was pregnant with me, there were no Doppler monitors listening for heartbeats and almost no prenatal care in Colombia. She read a book about natural childbirth that my grandmother had sent her and ate conscientiously. She wore sandals—Earth Shoes—that gave her toes wiggle room and her arches support. She told me once about an Indian she had met in the mountains who had never worn shoes. The Indian was a maid, who flapped around the house in flip-flops, the only footwear that would accommodate her spread-out toes, which had never been confined by leather or canvas. I remember my mother spreading out the fingers of her hand to demonstrate the appearance of this Indian's toes.

I pictured my mother reading her book on childbirth and feeling the first flutters of life, realizing that she was growing a baby inside her. I imagined her packing a satchel and boarding a bus to Cali, where she would live with a few American girls in a pink- or salmon-colored building with tile floors the Americans couldn't quite keep clean. She would have worn a thick wool ruana, hand-knit perhaps by a Guambiano woman. She might have removed her wedding ring made of a bent spoon handle, although this might have had more to do with prenatal water retention than marital discord. She wouldn't have been showing yet, her stomach just a little swell under her peasant blouse, and as the bus rattled down the Pan-American Highway and the climate shifted from mountain region to steamy valley, she would have shed the poncho, folded it as best she could and placed it with her luggage at her feet.

When my father and I had traveled by bus to Cali, our shoulders touched at each treacherous turn, and the closeness felt as foreign as the passing curves and the motorbikes that swerved around the bus. I was startled in my seat when the driver leaned on the horn, but the bleat was only meant to prod two brown cows that stood blocking the road. Despite the honking, the cows looked at the vehicle with bored, watery eyes before moving slowly out of the roadway.

Just as slowly I was lulled into complacency by the rocking of the bus and the smoky breeze that swept through the open windows. My father formed a sort of protective barrier between me and the other passengers. But when the bus shuddered to a stop on the side of the mountain, the gravel and asphalt highway crumbling into nothing at the edge of a cliff, and fingers of shrubs and vine invading the road, I felt a wave of panic and acrophobia. The unscheduled stop we had made on the way to Puracé was still fresh in my memory, and I looked for soldiers holding machine guns. There was no town in sight, no reason for a stop. My father had told me about the many traffic accidents—often fatal ones—that occurred on the narrow highway. I thought of road blocks and kidnappings, warfare and machine guns. As these thoughts raced through my head, I wanted to grip my father's hand. But I didn't move.

There was a clamber in the front of the bus, and a man boarded. He was loaded with, not rifles, but apples and pastries. As the bus started up again with a whine of gears, he swung his bags of *manzanas* and *pandebono* and shouted at the passengers: "Acá tenemos lo más rico. Toman algo." His accent was thick and guttural, and he clutched the seatbacks as he made his way toward the rear of the bus, looking for buyers of his wares. He had a scruffy beard and smelled of something ripe and primal. After a few passengers exchanged pesos for fruit and bread, the bus stopped again and left the man standing in the road behind us.

When the bus stopped a second time, a man with a scuffed guitar strapped to his back got on and headed down the aisle.

"The driver," my father explained to me as the busker started to play an out-of-key tune, "gets a kickback from these guys. That's why he stops."

When the guitar player got off, I wondered what happened to these peddlers when they disembarked miles from their starting points. They probably just kept going, I thought, because they had no other choice.

"Señoras y señores," the next man shouted, startling me with the tenor of his scratchy voice. He wore a brown wool poncho, probably similar to the one my mother would have worn, and carried a large bag filled with other little bags. "Using the spells of my ancestors," he announced in Spanish, "I can cure you. Here we have the potion to solve your problems in bed." He paused and winked at an overweight man with a mustache a few rows ahead of us. "A wart? Who has a wart? I will remove it before your eyes. These ancient recipes will heal you."

I watched him selling little sachets of herbs and grasses to the desperate, exchanging desires for coins, and was surprised by the brisk business he did, at the number of passengers willing to part with their money for a dream. Although, it occurred to me, that's what I had been doing. Exchanging some part of me for the dream of becoming a Colombian daughter.

A woman in a dress and cardigan stood in the aisle discussing a purchase with the peddler. My father leaned toward me and said in English, "Look at that. She believes in this bullshit."

He laughed and I joined in, laughing at these believers.

But as I watched the alleged healer walk up and down the aisles handing out magical bundles, I remembered that once, when I was seven or eight, I had seen fairies in my grandparents' apple tree. The branches, thick with pale pink blossoms, were heavy with a perfume as sweet as my grandmother's baking pies. Inside the blooms as light and fluffy as cotton candy, I saw fairies—little sparkles of light and motion. The wings, I thought then, were iridescent and transparent like cellophane mirages. I had chased them, swung on the branches like a Maypole, lifted my face to feel a warmth that didn't come from the sun or a fever. If I had been a churchgoer or a believer, I might have explained this with Bible verses and Holy Trinities, but I was a heathen child, already half in one world and half in another. I didn't feel the need to believe it in order for it to be true. I closed my eyes as if I knew, even then, that this was magic and I needed to will myself to remember every detail of this moment.

As the bus made its way into the lowlands of the Valle de Cauca and the heat intensified and I imagined my mother shedding her ruana, I didn't tell my father the story of the fairies. I didn't want to admit how much I wanted to believe in these cures and the magic of little pouches. When the magician was deposited on the side of the road, I wondered if he had a concoction to make me more Colombian, a poultice I could apply to become more my father's daughter, a charm that would rid me of my wonders and worries.

The pulsating of the sound waves pounded in my ears, and the wall alongside the exam table felt like it was closing in on me. The tile flooring, the drop ceiling, the doctor's lab coat were all white, reminding me of my father's fascination with shading and perspective. There's a joke familiar to all Minnesota schoolkids in which you produce a blank piece of paper and ask, "What's this?" The answer, during which giggling ensues, is that it is a picture of a polar bear in a snowstorm. White on white, easily confused with nothing.

The doctor shifted the probe across my belly, and the volume increased, faded, then increased again. "Sounds healthy."

I knew I was supposed to smile, but I was suddenly horrified. I had, I realized, a being inside me. I was possessed, haunted. What was this thing, I wondered, who had taken up residence in my uterus? I knew I should be crying tears of joy, that I ought to be relieved to receive this news of a healthy fetus, to witness the miracle of life in the form of sound waves. But I couldn't muster anything more than a half smile to placate the doctor. And I wasn't sure how I felt about adding yet another new person to my life, another object to my orbit.

My brother had a surprise, he said when I called him. We had been back to visit him several times in the three years since we moved to Minnesota, and he had even once agreed to come to Minneapolis and see the fall foliage. While Dave and I planned our pre-baby visit to California, my brother hadn't called it a secret, but he hadn't given me an inkling of what it was either. Of course, I also had a surprise—my own secret—in this new life that was growing inside me. Dave and I were telling our family and friends one by one, little by little, but I was caught in that time period when it isn't apparent to onlookers that you have a tiny zygote percolating inside. My mother had spent this first part of her pregnancy with the other girls in Cali, and then she had gone home to Minnesota. Her parents were happy to take her in. When she opened gifts of tiny socks and little bibs at a baby shower, I could imagine that even then she had not decided whether she would go back to Colombia at all.

When Dave and I arrived at Silas's house in the Bay Area, his new girlfriend opened the door.

"Renzo is at work," she said. Milenka was from Peru and spoke accented English, rolling the R in my brother's first name, his given name. In *One Hundred Years of Solitude*, Aureliano Buendía leaves a wake of illegitimate sons wherever his warring takes him. And the sons are given Aureliano as their first name and, like my brother, their mothers' last names. Each one comes back to find him when they are tall, broad, strong young men. The senior Aureliano doesn't really know what to do with these dozens of sons, but his mother makes them all go to Ash Wednesday mass, where they are anointed with a cross of ashes on their foreheads, a permanent mark they wear for the rest of their lives.

We followed Milenka inside the house. She was petite and pretty with long hair and red lipstick.

"Maybe the surprise is that they're getting married," Dave whispered to me. I wasn't sure that was the answer; Silas's mother had never married either his father or his brother's father. I couldn't really imagine him wearing a black tuxedo with his black hair slicked back, his goatee trimmed, a nervous flush to his cheeks.

For dinner that night, Silas made spaghetti and garlic bread. I was over the worst of the nausea of the first trimester, but many smells still made my stomach turn. I helped by sitting at the table cutting vegetables for a salad. At least I thought I was helping until I sliced my finger instead of a carrot. In their bathroom, I opened cupboards and cabinets looking for Band-Aids. When I swung the mirror back I saw, on a crowded glass shelf, a bottle of prenatal vitamins. Could it be? I wondered. I quickly closed the door and smiled at myself in the toothpaste-splattered mirror.

Silas and I are not marked as children of our father, not in any way that can be seen from the outside. But we are marked inside with something just as indelible. We are siblings and yet lost; we are offspring from the same loins and yet strangers; we are intimates and yet hidden. That he and I might be having children at the same time felt preposterous. It went beyond the stuff of fairy tales and magical realism and delved into the arena of falsehoods and lies.

When I came back from the bathroom, Silas held up a bottle of cabernet. "Wine, Sis?"

I instinctively put a hand over my belly. Now that I was growing this alien inside me, I could understand better my mother's urges during those first few months, and I wondered whether she had been trying to escape her husband or me, the child-to-be. At the first flutters of movement in my uterus, I didn't feel a thrill of excitement. Before I grew accustomed to it, the sensation of being occupied was too strong; the feeling of being followed and watched haunted me. When the thing inside me flipped and flopped, I frequently rested my hand on my abdomen as if I could calm this being from the outside. "I'm good, thanks."

"Well," Dave said as we sat down to dinner.

"What's your surprise?" I asked even before anyone had taken a bite.

Silas and Milenka looked at each other. I held my breath for the news that I knew was coming.

"We're having a baby."

Dave and I started laughing, shaking our heads, laughing.

"So are we."

And then we were all laughing, nearly crying.

"Have you told Renzo?"

"I called him on Easter."

"No. Way."

"You called the same day?"

And the tears from laugher were mingled with tears of sorrow, tears of what could have been. I pictured my father in his house in Popayán, the city noisy and crowded from the famous *Semana Santa* parades and processions that draw tourists from around the world during Easter week. He would have declined any invitations to church or Ceci's parents' house and opted instead for a quiet noon meal at home beside the canaries that gathered in the courtyard.

When the telephone rang and his live-in maid answered, he would have taken the receiver from her hand. The phone in the dining room was an old rotary style, a greenish-gray model. He would have said, "¿Quién es?" and heard his son's voice. And when he heard the news, the news that at that point still made Silas sick to his stomach if he thought about it too much, he cried. He wept and congratulated this young man. He would have promised not to tell me. And then my father would have gone back to his meal, perhaps already envisioning a new painting he would begin, one that was inspired by new life. When the phone rang again, he might have been expecting a call from Ceci, but when he answered and it was his daughter, he would have wanted to tell me about this baby that would be born. And so when I told him we were having a baby, he didn't cry. This time he laughed, he laughed as much as we were laughing now with the ridiculousness of life.

"Due date?"

"October seventh. You?"

"October twenty-eighth."

"Twins!"

And the world and its marvels and mistakes opened up. We clinked glasses (that contained no alcohol) and laughed and chose to be in this moment of joy. The long and convoluted road that had led to a brother and sister four months apart now pointed toward future cousins who would grow up knowing one another. Between Silas and me, we were able to break the cycle of secrets. With a trick of timing and a twist of chance, there would be two children closer in age than seemed possible.

24

THE ILLEGITIMATE SONS of Aureliano Buendía—the large, handsome young men marked with the cross of ash—were all murdered. This happens in the latter half of *One Hundred Years of Solitude* and is told as matter-of-factly as their births. But birth and death are nothing alike, I thought, as the pain of labor seeped in during the predawn hours on a Saturday in late October. Death is the end of pain, and birth, I realized, is only the beginning. A rope tightened around my abdomen and lower back as if my organs had been taken over by a complex system of pulleys and ratchets. The urgency and intensity of contractions felt like a civil war inside me, like treason, one part of me betraying the desires of the other.

"I don't want to do this," I told Dave, whose breath gagged me with the smell of milk and cereal. The bedroom walls we had painted last summer closed in on me with their beigeness, and the sheets of our marital bed were too hot and too wrinkled. Every movement awoke the pain inside me, beside me. "You do it."

But he couldn't and I had to.

When we arrived at the hospital in Minneapolis, I was already exhausted from the relentless pounding and pulsing in my lower back. While Dave parked the car, I waited alone in the high-ceilinged foyer. There were no other patients on this gray morning, and I was left to suffer alone with only a passing janitor for company.

The antiseptic smells and the flickering fluorescent lights reminded me of the time, nearly a decade ago, when my grandfather had been in the hospital with a blood infection. When I had seen him in a hospital gown on the cold white sheets of the bed, he had looked old and fragile. The table next to his bed was stacked with *National Geographics* and *National History* magazines, which he carted with him everywhere in a leather satchel. I sat talking with him while my mother and grandmother went to the cafeteria.

"Did you know, honey," he had said, "that the world was created on your birthday?"

I didn't say anything as he fumbled with the glossy pages of a magazine, his hand wrinkled and spotted with brown as if chocolate ice cream had melted over his knuckles. A large white bandage covered the catheter hub that carried antibiotics to his bloodstream.

"This bishop, James Ussher, figured out the exact date of this beginning of the world. He spent his life calculating dates for everything. The twenty-third of October, your birthday. Well, a different year, of course. Four thousand four B.C."

I nodded. My grandfather had been telling me stories all my life, and I had believed them all.

"So you were born on the day the world was created, honey."

I leaned on the counter of the maternity floor's registration desk, letting the pulsing seize and suspend me.

"Name?" said the woman behind the sliding glass window.

I glared at her as another contraction gripped me. We were two days away from the beginning of the world, but it felt like the end.

Her hands were poised above the keyboard, and Dave stepped in front of me and gave her my vital information while I gripped the edge of the counter.

We were shown into a small dark room with a bed in the center like a throne.

"You can put this on," a medical assistant said, handing Dave a white, flowered hospital gown.

Dave helped me out of my sweatpants and onto the bed. I concentrated on my most self-centered survival. Fuck. How had my mother done this with two men drinking whiskey beside her? Jesus fucking

Christ. Breathe in. Breathe out. Curse. Holy shit. I wasn't thinking about family or my mother or my father or the son that had been born to Silas and Milenka a week before. I wasn't thinking about some bullshit miracle of bringing a new life into the world. I wasn't even thinking about the world anymore. Fuck. I was thinking only about me.

"If you want an epidural for the pain, we need to do it now," said the nurse who checked on me.

We had talked about not using meds. Dave and I had researched the options in our careful studious ways. He looked at me for a cue.

"Now," I said.

I appreciated the speed with which the nurse left to carry out my demands.

Soon another nurse walked us down a hallway to the labor room, which had a view of the industrial buildings in that part of the city. The streets below were gloomy and vacant, and I felt like the last person in the world, the queen bee, the one who had to perform the duty of populating the colony again.

"You're going to sit on the edge of the bed," the anesthesiologist told me, "and lean forward while I insert the catheter into your back."

"He's going to have to leave," I said between contractions, pointing at Dave. "He faints."

Back when we still lived in Madison and were dating, the two of us irresponsible college sweethearts, Dave and I had gone to see *Pulp Fiction* in a crowded movie theater. We were in the middle of the back row, where we had an unobstructed view of the screen. In the film, Uma Thurman's character has a drug overdose, and the prescribed remedy is a shot of adrenaline, administered straight to the heart. John Travolta's character holds a huge syringe over her, its five-inch needle dripping, and then plunges it in. Next to me, Dave had shuddered and then slumped forward, head to knees.

"Let's go," I had whispered. "Do you have to throw up?" I shook his arm, and he bolted upright again.

"I'm fine," he whispered back. "I just fainted."

So in the labor room, I didn't want him there while the needle was being inserted into the epidural space in my spine. I didn't want any distractions from me; I wanted all the attention, all care focused on me. I was the only one in the room, the only child.

When the anesthetic took effect and I was feeling only the force of the contractions, not their stabbing, I was hungry. I told the nurse, "I want a steak and a baked potato."

But she said I wasn't allowed to eat.

"A glass of wine?" I tried.

The nurse ignored me. She came and went, preparing equipment and instruments just out of my sight. Dave held my hand and then stood by the window to watch the gray day. Then the pain, which had been dulled, slowly and inexplicably returned inch by inch, first a nagging ache, then a sharp throbbing that radiated from my lower back and down my legs. In sixth-grade science class I collected insects, killed them in jars of alcohol, and pinned them to a sheet of white and crumbly Styrofoam. Monarchs, dragonflies, moths. This was what happened to creatures that obeyed their homing instincts. I had suspended the dead insects on colorful ball-head pins, and now, as the twisting spasms tried to contort my body, I felt as if I had been captured, tied down by tubes and monitors, like a round beetle.

"Keep breathing," the nurse said.

"Do you want music?" Dave asked. He had made a CD of soothing songs in preparation for this moment. Adrian Legg, Leo Kottke, and Yo-Yo Ma. He popped the CD into the boom box he had hauled in from the car. Quiet acoustic guitars and gentle moans of cello and strumming mandolins circled and spun. The pain seemed worse, amplified by having been absent for a time. I closed my eyes, listened to the music, breathed. I let the whole thing wash over me, and then I opened my eyes, suddenly annoyed at Dave's ministrations and the mandates from the nurse.

"Turn that thing off," I told Dave.

I turned to the nurse next. "Do you know," I said as rudely as I could, "that wallpaper border is the ugliest thing I have ever seen."

The border was blues and pinks, colors left over from the early nineties, insipid and faded. It felt like an insult to what I was trying to do here.

But the nurse only laughed. "When you fill out the evaluation about your care here, be sure to mention the wallpaper," she said.

I almost laughed then, too, but another twist of my contracting uterus caught my breath and seemed to rob it from me. The pain was intense and alive. It controlled me. I thought about dying. Did, I wondered, the universe contort and convulse like this when it was created?

"Push," the doctor said after hours—who knew how many—of this writhing and wishing.

"Bear down," said the nurse.

I thought of my grandmother making bread, folding and kneading the dough with well-floured hands. My whole body felt like that dough, the pain clawing at me. I wasn't thinking about steaks anymore. I lifted my knees to my chest and thought about the movie scenes of actresses pretending to give birth. I imitated their faces, but I wasn't sure what I was actually supposed to do. I felt like a character in a story.

"How's your pain level?" the nurse asked, looking not at me but at the pump beside me. "On a scale of one to ten?"

"A twenty," I said.

She fiddled with the dials and buttons, the magical increments that were supposed to give me relief. Even with this pain, I was grateful to be in a clean hospital room, in my own reality, and not on a hammock in a jungle like Úrsula Buendía in *One Hundred Years of Solitude*.

"How about now?"

I felt the same; the same snaking, sneaking pain lashed at me. "A nineteen," I said because I didn't want to be uncooperative.

"Okay, we can see the head," the doctor said. "Black hair."

I had also come out with black hair. Black hair and dark eyes in an impossibly round face. Round like the sun. I was the sun, I thought.

Then the doctor said, "Looks like the baby is posterior."

"What does that mean?" Dave asked, letting go of my hand for a moment.

"Face up. We need to do a cesarean."

"No!" I was adamant. "I can feel everything," I cried.

The doctor looked at me. It was nearly midnight on a Saturday, and I wondered where she would have rather been at that moment. Where would I have rather been. She sighed, and I knew that I wasn't unique. The new mother who didn't want surgery after fourteen hours of labor. She'd seen all this before.

"Do you want this baby to come out?" the doctor asked at last.

My favorite image from my father's artwork is a dove perched on a barbed wire, these two opposing symbols captured together in one graceful arc. He had designed the image in pencil and black ink and then transferred it to the digital world, where he worked it, kneaded it, shaped it, and colored it. The work was part of a series for an exhibit he had done called *Kosombia,* named for both the bloody Kosovo War in the late 1990s and the decades of violence of his own country. The paintings captured the horror of both places with falling helicopters and smashed red roof tiles. But the dove on the barbed wire was my favorite image, combining so perfectly two dichotomous paradigms. Violence and life. Peace and danger.

My father put both of these thoughts side by side, and I wondered whether simultaneously holding opposing thoughts in your head was a sign of genius or insanity. I didn't know if I was capable of that kind of cognitive dissonance, if I had the same ability, the same genius. But I did know that perhaps I had the insanity, because even as I knew this baby would be born soon if not right now, I wanted to keep this new life inside me.

"Let's get her prepped," the doctor said to the nurses. And it was all out of my control, not my choice to make.

I was transferred to a gurney, and Dave was led away to change into scrubs and eat peanut butter sandwiches meant to fortify him. He was gone, and I was being wheeled down a corridor, the white tubes of light on the ceiling passing in front of my vision like telephone poles down a highway. And I suddenly remembered watching the lights pass over me on the way to my bladder surgery. I was three years old again, wondering what was going on, wondering where my mother was. Afraid and at the same time not afraid, willing to let someone—anyone—take care of me.

Once in the operating room, the anesthesiologist, who had just come on duty, discovered that the catheter had slipped out of the epidural space. Without the anesthetic running through the spine, I had been experiencing unmedicated labor as if I had been foolish enough to do the whole thing as naturally as my mother and grandmother had done.

"I can't have surgery without something," I said. I envisioned a knife, a large kitchen knife, cutting through the flesh of my distended belly.

"We're going to have to do a spinal block," she told me. "I have to let you know that this isn't ideal, doing a block after an epidural."

I sat on the edge of the operating table, hugging the obstetrician, my swollen feet dangling over the white tile. If I had grown up in Colombia, if I had married a Colombian man and gone into labor in a Colombian hospital, would I be getting a spinal block now? I wondered. Behind me, the anesthesiologist poked and prodded at my lower back even as contractions gripped me. I thought of my mother in labor in what was then a fairly primitive hospital in Popayán, two hundred miles from a big city, three thousand miles from her mother. The needle was going into my back, but it couldn't seem to locate the magical subarachnoid space. So I kept talking as if the talking, the storytelling, would fortify me and keep me alive.

"My husband has a big head," I told the doctor as I clung to her neck, breathing in her smell of antibacterial foam. "We can never find hats to fit him."

The ob-gyn looked down at me. "Never marry someone with a big head."

At last the spinal block took hold, and they laid me down on the table, a nurse at my head, her hands outstretched as if to catch me should I fall. I heard the doctors and nurses and knew there was a bed and warming lamp for whatever would be pulled from me. And then I felt myself going numb—no, that's not what it was; numbness suggests a sensation, and I was experiencing a complete absence of feeling. The anti-feeling started at my stomach and lower back and moved its way up. My fingers, my arms, my chest. It moved into my ears, my chin, my cheeks. It began to take hold of my breathing, my mouth.

"Help," I cried out. "I can't breathe."

It was a bad dream, the kind where you try to scream but no sound comes out, the kind where you try to run but your feet won't move.

"Help," I said in a whisper, all feebleness. And then I wasn't thinking anymore, not about babies or mothers or galaxies.

"Keep breathing," the nurse said. "It's okay."

And then everything went out.

It was like trying to swim through black oil, that coming out of the netherworld. Like a surreal dream that feels like reality. I was reluctant to open my eyes, as if it would be easier to just fall back and let myself plunge into nothingness.

I heard a voice from somewhere.

"It's a girl," the voice said. But I didn't know what those words meant.

Were those the same words my mother had heard when I was born at five thirty in the morning when the sky above Popayán was still dark? Had she felt like this when she first saw me, a tiny infant, wrapped like an airmail package?

"It's a girl," Dave said.

"No, it's not," I said, and I opened my eyes, was blinded by lights. Lights like the big bang of the universe, the explosion of atoms and particles that created the world as we eventually came to know it. *In the beginning there was light.* Weren't those the words in the Bible?

"Look," I heard him say. But I didn't see anything, just shapes and shadows of the recovery room. I closed my eyes again.

I awoke again later when the nurse brought my baby to me, laid her in my arms. We were in a new room, and Dave was asleep in the fold-down chair beside my bed. With the glow of the hall light, I could see the baby's face, small and round. A cherub nose like all babies have, slits of eyes, thin lips. Her hands were little claws, impossibly small like a fairy's. I looked up to see the clock on the wall tick to four in the morning.

"This is my new life," I said. Or maybe I just thought it.

The next day my throat was scratchy from the intubation. When the doctors and nurses came to take my blood pressure and monitor my urinary output, they didn't tell me how lucky I was. They didn't tell me how controversial it was to administer a spinal block following an epidural. They didn't mention that patients can die from what I later learned was called accidental total spinal analgesia. They didn't tell me how dangerous this would have been if my mother, in 1974 in the provincial Colombian hospital, had experienced similar troubles while giving birth to me. They watched me carefully, though, gave me opioids, and tended my staples.

My mother was the first of the visitors to arrive, and she looked so normal in her coat and gloves. Somehow I had expected that everything and everyone would be different now. But my mother was still my mother. She leaned over the bassinet in the hospital room and scooped up the baby. I watched my mother cradle my daughter's head, hold her at arm's length, both of them trying to focus on the other.

"What's the name you chose?"

Dave stood, puffed his chest a bit. "Meet Sylvia," he said.

"Well," my mother said. And there was a split second when I wondered if she felt betrayed, if we had done the right thing naming our child for the town in Colombia (albeit spelled wrong). The town where I had been conceived (and where Silas had also been created). But she looked at the baby in her arms and smiled. "Beautiful."

Then the baby began to fuss, and Dave took over. He laid the infant in the bassinet to change her diaper.

"Look at those toes," my mother said, watching. While Dave practiced his new skill, she took hold of one of Sylvia's feet, held it in her hand. The feet were wrinkled and pink, they were padded on the tops and bottoms, and my mother looked like she wanted to put one in her mouth. "They are just like yours were. We used to call them little tamales."

Later that day my grandparents arrived at the hospital. They brought champagne.

"Nursing mothers shouldn't have any champagne," the brusque nurse taking my blood pressure said. "No amount of alcohol is safe." Her nasally voice sounded like a recording from a neonatal instructional film.

"But it's her birthday!" my mother cried. She poured the sparkling wine into plastic hospital cups.

The day after giving birth to my own child, and it was my birthday. The beginning of the world.

"Happy birthday to you," sang my family, my grandmother's wobbly harmonization coming in for the finale. Even though I already understood that I had been usurped, I still had one more day of being serenaded.

The tiny creature lay in my arms as they sang, her fists clenched as if she were still hanging on for dear life. My breasts were engorged and tight with milk, and the baby's mouth was so tiny. I latched her toothless gums around my nipple, and I felt less like the center of the universe and more like the center of *her* universe. In Spanish, to give birth is *dar luz*. To give light. I looked down at her, this girl who would be, I hoped, my light. I wished that I could already grasp the significance of this moment, of this new life. But it was too soon for that. I sipped the champagne, and the cold bubbles shocked and startled.

25

THOSE FIRST DAYS WERE LONG, and the nights were even longer. In a fog, in a funk, in a *fracaso* of sleeplessness, I thought of the nighttime glow of the Spanish-style San Jose Hospital, the hospital in the old part of Popayán in which my mother had given birth. The building had been destroyed in an earthquake in the 1980s and rebuilt as it had always been. Could everything, I wondered, be returned to normal with enough work?

"I was born there," I had told María Fernanda and her sister María Alejandra when they pointed out the hospital on my first visit to Colombia.

Ceci's nieces (whom I could never keep straight) took me on a tour of Popayán. El Morro, the Humilladero Bridge, Parque Caldas, the recently built Pueblito Patojo. Someone's ex-boyfriend drove a little blue car, and there were a few other cousins or friends packed into the sticky back seat. As we joked and laughed and the twenty-something kids in the car got louder and rowdier, María Fernanda (or maybe it was María Alejandra) turned to me and said, "You're speaking like a native now. Your Spanish is perfect, Anika."

"Es un milagro," María Alejandra said.

"If it's a miracle, we need to go thank the Virgen," María Fernanda said.

I knew my Spanish-speaking ability wasn't a miracle; I knew it was a result of years of study, a semester of college-level Spanish in Spain, and the intense immersion I was experiencing in Colombia. But if they wanted to believe in a miracle, I had thought, why stop them?

"Let's go to Iglesia de Santo Domingo."

I started to laugh because I thought she was joking about giving thanks, but the driver had already turned the car, embarking on uncharted territory. I was familiar with Jesus and his cross, Noah and his ark, but my religious education hadn't gone much further than that. While my childhood friends were at Lutheran Sunday school, I was exploring the woods with my mother, watching early dandelions peek their heads through brown grass, studying chickadees and red squirrels. My mother had taken me to church for the occasional wedding or funeral, but what she believed in was nature. A red-winged blackbird spotted on a highway overpass was reason to pause and reflect on the enormity of the world. An orange sunset over a glassy lake could stall dinner. An owl illuminated by our headlights was cause to wake a sleeping child.

"Let's go see la fantasma," someone in the car said.

La fantasma? The ghost? I wasn't sure I had translated that correctly, despite my newfound and "perfect" Spanish.

The sun's last rays cast shadows of rolling curves on milky buildings as the driver careened around corners and honked at the scooters that whizzed by. He then came to an abrupt halt halfway on the sidewalk near a small plaza. A dusty gray fountain stood in the middle, and across from this were the doors of a church.

Even in the twilight I could make out its arches and spires; the Iglesia de Santo Domingo was my idea of a church. I had seen so many churches during my time in Spain (French, Italian, Spanish), and they had all been old and dignified like this one. Despite my mother's religious reluctance, when she married my stepfather he decided that our new blended family needed to attend a church, a Presbyterian church on a bland suburban street with a short-cropped lawn and spirea for landscaping. The building was late-1960s or early-1970s blond wood and turquoise upholstery—everything the antithesis of this postcolonial church.

"This is where the ghost woman lives," María Fernanda explained to me as I followed her out of the car. The others were already crossing the plaza, but I hung back a moment, watching her black braid swing against her back. After all, I didn't believe in ghosts. I knew that spirits did not walk the cobbled streets or aisles of churches. I certainly had never seen a ghost at the Presbyterian church. And if there had been one, I would have seen it when I stole a Bible from one of the pews. A Revised Standard Version, it had been dedicated to the church from some long-forgotten family. I took it home and thumbed through its gold-edged pages and found the Psalms, black and white text that could be touched. *Save me, oh God, for the waters have come up to my neck.* I marked the page and found comfort in the words, although whether they were written by the hand of God was something for believers to decide. I was an American and a pragmatist and, standing in this square in South America, I hung on—desperately, perhaps—to what was real: a carload of twenty-somethings, the lingering smell of motor oil, the scent of lemons from a tree hidden in a courtyard somewhere.

"Vámonos," someone called, and I ran to catch up with María Fernanda.

As we walked across the plaza, she told me about the ghost woman. She told me that you could hear the ghost singing mass in Latin and that some people go crazy after seeing her. As I listened, my mind wandered to Allende, Borges, García Márquez. I had read enough magical realism to know that Latin America is fond of the imaginary, the line between real and fantasy blurry. Just like the division between political protest and drug smuggling is permeable, the demarcation between good and bad is changeable, malleable, and fluid. Ancient family trees intertwine and heal where they have been hacked down. Friends can become enemies as easily as acquaintances can become family. The line tends to be a moving target, and instead of questioning it's better to just accept.

When we approached the baroque building, I stood behind my guides as they crept up to the huge doors. If my father had been with us, he would have ignored the religious meaning of the church but pointed out the lines, the movement, the architecture. The hinges, darkened with age, were out of a movie set, worn by use and rusted in places where relentless winter rains had pounded. My companions were dwarfed by the massive slabs of wood and heavy iron handles.

"It's locked; we can't go in," I heard.

"Look through there." The driver of the small blue car pointed to the space between the doors.

One of the boys leaned in, his black hair brushing the wood. "I can see something!" he cried.

There was a scuffle as everyone tried to look through the crack, but I stood back a bit, waiting for the childishness to end, not wanting to take up the space that should be allotted to a believer.

And then: "¡La veo!" someone shouted. "I see her!"

I was the last one to move toward the doors. Someone pushed me forward, as if sensing my reluctance. As I peeked through the space between the doors of the church, I saw light. Light as if from a candle, many candles, as if seen through a camera's soft-focus filter. I pressed my forehead against the rough wood to get a better look. I could feel the splinters scratch my face, and the damp cold of the mountain air played at the back of my neck. I focused on the shadow of a black boot. The rough skirt of a wool habit. A hunched form shuffling past the candlelight.

The swirl of Spanish surrounded me, and the pungent scent of the old town tickled my nostrils. Colombia was all around me, below me, in me, through me. Hundreds of years of *indios* and *Católicos* pushed against me. The songs of the slaves that had built the church and laid each brick echoed in my ears. I could feel the Colombian blood pulsing through my veins.

My eyes stung with the strain of keeping them open. I was afraid to blink in case I missed something. And then, just when I was beginning to be sure—absolutely positive—that I had seen something, laughter erupted from the voices behind me, and I closed my eyes for an instant. Before following the group that was heading back to the car, I peered through the crack in the door again. I couldn't see anything. My heart pounded out the Colombian blood, and I was once again American. It was dark in the chapel, no light, no figure, no glow. Just a quiet, nighttime, shuttered *iglesia* waiting for morning mass.

We climbed back into the little car. As we drove away, María Fernanda whispered, "Did you see her?"

Like my parents, I believe in what I can see. A hawk in the clouds, a shadow reflected on a frozen lake. A dark line of paint or a soft brush of pencil. A heavy wooden door; cold iron hinges; a laughing, teasing group of young people; a ghost woman.

"Sí," I said, leaning back into the blue vinyl seat.

26

I STUMBLED OUT OF BED and scooped up my screaming baby. Night after night. At first, I made an effort of inhaling the scent of her soft fontanel and trying to cherish the moment.

But I didn't have the heart for it. Survival seemed questionable, miracles impossible.

When Dave went back to work and I was alone with the baby all day, the days grew just as long as the nights. At times, the three of us—me, Sylvia, and the cat—would nap on our bed in the afternoons. I watched my fitfully sleeping baby and gently wheezing tabby and thought about how many years I had loved this feline and how I didn't know this human-child at all. This new parenting was like having a stranger instantly become part of your family.

Of course, strangers becoming family was nothing new. Silas sent me pictures of a round-headed infant with big eyes and round cheeks. My nephew. More family. I felt as if I were drowning in family, unsure of what to grab on to.

During these times, my mother came to help as much as she could. She was more worried about me than her new grandchild, and now I wonder if she was so attentive not only because she was my mother but because she knew what it felt like to struggle with an infant. If she did, she didn't let on. She simply said, "You lie down. We'll take care of her."

Once, just once, I felt as desperate as she might have. After she closed my bedroom door and took the baby downstairs, I stared at the slit of light from the hall slicing the blackness. I listened to her and Dave in the kitchen, the murmur of their voices interrupted occasionally with the foreign whimpering of an infant. My breasts swelled with milk at the sound, and I rolled over and wept. I turned away from the light and lay on my side, facing the dark window, the window above my neighbor's asphalt driveway two stories below. I thought of how easily the sash slid up, how the screen popped out.

Escape can take many forms. For my mother, it hadn't been a twenty-foot drop but a three-thousand-mile plane ride. I thought of her whisking me away, first to her family's cabin, then to the care of Mary Jean, my grandmother's best friend, who lived in an innocuous suburban rambler that had synthetic carpeting and laminate countertops. I remembered Mary Jean's thick eyelashes, gravelly smoker's laugh, and unflappable manner and realized she had been the perfect accomplice.

"But we didn't know that she had you," my grandmother had said when I was a teenager and hearing this story for the first time. "No one could know where you were so that if they asked, we could honestly say we didn't know."

I tried to imagine myself, a wailing toddler, in the arms of a stranger. I tried to imagine the lengths my mother went so that she could keep me.

"It was cloak-and-dagger stuff," my grandfather had told me. "We watched Renzo and the consul drive around the neighborhood looking for you." I pictured my grandparents standing just behind the curtain in their dining room, leaning slightly against the seagrass wallpaper. I imagined a black government sedan prowling the street that circled the neighborhood, passing the Eight Pond (named for its shape) and the vacant lot (where we could always find butterflies) and the storm drain that collected deep puddles to splash in each spring. I pictured my father hidden behind tinted-glass windows peering out at the post–World War II split-levels painted dismal hues of brown and gray and tan. I imagined the invisible scars the vehicle must have left on the streets I would later run and walk and bike on. "Spooky," my grandfather said.

In the end, it turned out that my mother had planned well. A U.S. court, at a time when mothers were almost always guaranteed guardianship, granted her sole custody and charged my father one hundred dollars, a sum he never paid.

"I remember the day he said goodbye to you," my grandmother said. "He took you to feed the ducks at the Eight Pond. I felt sorry for him, so we let him take you down there."

As my grandmother told me this, I could picture the grassy shore that sloped down from the road above. The pond was technically on private property, but all the kids of the neighborhood fed the ducks in the summer and skated on the ice in the winter, possession trumping borders. I imagined me, a little girl with blunt-cut bangs and elbows dimpled with baby fat, perched beside my father on the neatly cut grass of the bank. Perhaps I pointed a chubby finger at the ducks swimming in the pond.

"Pato," I might have said, one of my few words.

"Pato," my father might have repeated.

Perhaps I watched a duck send ripples across the water, not yet knowing that they were mallards, a species native to North America, that the female's inconspicuous mottled brown feathers help her to blend into her surroundings. Maybe I pointed to the drake that swam in figure eights around his mate, resplendent in iridescent green, his head appearing blue, then emerald, his neck ringed in white, like the line left after a wedding band is surreptitiously slipped into a pocket.

To my father, the Eight Pond perhaps looked, for just a moment, less like something quantifiable and more like two ample breasts. Or maybe he remembered, a fact dredged up from his Catholic childhood in Colombia, that eight is the symbol for resurrection and new life.

"I will send you a duck, my dear," my father might have said to me. "A pato for you." He sent me one of the wooden ducks he designed and painted to sell to art collectors. A life-size mallard hen, a faithful imitation of the real thing. For many years, the bird's glass eyes watched over me, and now the wooden duck, a replica in vivid color, sat atop a shelf in my baby's room, where Dave would pace with her nestled against his shoulder. Sylvia's little pudgy hand would slip into his shirt pocket, and our baby looked so content in the arms of her father, watching the world from his height. I wondered what it meant to take a child away from a father.

"We liked Renzo," my grandmother had said.

"It just wasn't meant to be," my grandfather had finished.

Maybe it wasn't meant to be, my having a father and mother. But even if that fate had been my past, it didn't have to dictate my future.

At my six-week postpartum appointment, the nurse wrapped a blood pressure cuff around my upper arm. From the car seat propped on the floor of the exam room, Sylvia studied her surroundings with big baby-blue eyes.

"You know what I think," the nurse said as she pumped the cuff. "I think babies are wasted on new mothers. We should have them the other way around: start out with eighteen-year-olds and then, when you're my age, end up with tiny babies. I have all the energy in the world to cuddle a baby."

She smiled, the creases at the corners of her eyes and mouth soft and comforting. I tried to return the smile, but I had done very little smiling in the past few weeks. I had wanted this—a baby, this life— but in the middle of the night as I stumbled around the nursery that used to be an office, I wondered why I had done this to myself.

"How are you doing today?" the doctor asked when she came in and had complimented the alertness of the baby.

"Tired."

"Very tired?"

I had never experienced exhaustion like what I was living since the birth of this baby. That my parents had thought a baby would save their marriage was proof of their foolish optimism, the same optimism that led to their marriage in the first place. Dave and I had been struggling blurry-eyed for these first weeks, barely talking, hardly touching except to hand off the bundle of spit-up and blankets. Parenthood doesn't bring you closer; just because you share blood and ancestry doesn't mean you form an instant bond. It would be so easy to become like two sides in a civil war, each fighting for survival.

"So tired."

The doctor checked the smile-shaped slice across my abdomen, proof that this thing had been wrenched from me. She palpated the area, but all I could feel was the presence of her hands.

"It's numb," I said. There was a scar, but I had no feeling.

"The incision for a C-section severs some nerves," the doctor explained. "They'll grow back eventually, but it can take years for the numbness to go away."

Tears that seemed always to be ready started dripping down my cheeks.

As the doctor pulled a Kleenex from a box, the baby startled at the sound, her eyes gone wide, her face scrunched and ready for wailing.

"This is so hard," I said.

"Do you ever feel like hurting your baby?" Her hand was poised over my chart as if deciding which box to check.

I shook my head as my infant wiggled her feet instead of crying.

"Do you ever feel like hurting yourself?"

I shook my head again. That night in the dark of my bedroom, the quiet had eventually lulled me to sleep, and I hadn't looked at windows like that again.

"Do you feel like getting on a plane and not coming back?"

My father had once designed way-finding signage for an airport in South America. As a graphic designer and artist, he was skilled at making the mundane visually appealing, at looking at flow and movement in new ways. It was comforting to think that somewhere there was a terminal where people followed his suggested path, looked up when they were lost and read his boldly lettered signs. I wished that he had left similar signs for me to follow.

The day I departed Colombia almost twenty years ago, I remember sitting next to my suitcase as a uniformed security guard strolled through the area with a dog straining at its leash. The dog sniffed each bag, each passenger, each cumbersome shoe. The dog was checking for drugs, but I wondered what else he could smell, what scent each person carried away with him. I wished that I had packed the smell of my father's cigarettes, the aroma of frying *plátanos,* the must of old photographs, the scent of lemons. If I had never left, never got on that plane, never married Dave, I thought, perhaps I would be living in Colombia, where my father and Ceci would take care of me, where a maid would bring me slices of mango and my father would treat me like a child.

I thought of the preposterousness of air travel, the defying of gravity and fear, and both of those things sounded wonderful. To board a plane and never come back sounded like a wonderful, split-second fantasy.

"Yes," I told the doctor.

But this was life, real life. And it was mine.

"Let's get you on some Zoloft," the doctor said.

And I wondered if antidepressants could have saved my parents' marriage, if modern medicine could have altered my life's trajectory. The number of points where a life can diverge is infinite.

27

WHEN, AT SIXTEEN MONTHS, Sylvia finally pulled herself up on the coffee table and began to take tentative steps, I bought her a miniature pair of soft-soled Mary Janes, brown leather with pink and white polka dots. My mother had been adamant about foot health, and so the shoes were not only adorable, they were also specially designed for growing infant feet. I had grown up wearing sturdy Buster Browns and lace-up athletic shoes, but once there was a pair of hand-me-down black patent leather shoes. She must have given in to my desires after I found the Mary Janes at the bottom of some bag of clothes other families passed along to single mothers.

"Can I wear them to day care?" I had asked. I was five, almost six, about to start kindergarten in the fall. And she had let me wear the shoes to preschool. But when one of the straps of the used shoes broke off, the preschool teacher stapled it back on—with the sharp prongs pointed inward. I remember the tetanus shot I had to get that evening, as memorable perhaps as Sylvia falling on the sidewalk during her first outing in her new shoes.

But even after the vaccination and the bloody chin, we parents are indulgent. I remember that one year she bought me a coveted pair of two-toned saddle shoes. My father, too, bought me shoes. A pair of sandals in Cali. And after choosing for me a pair with soft brown leather straps and low wooden heels, we had walked the river path along the Río Cauca where birds of paradise and hibiscus bloomed.

"How long are we going to walk?" I had asked him as the leather began to rub.

"Do you need a rest, my dear?" he had asked, and we sat on a bench while I eased the shoes away from my growing blisters.

"Come, rest," he said, and we sat watching the birds of paradise sway in the humid breeze.

"See that?" my father had said, pointing to an impossibly large and knotted tree behind us. He had been pointing out plants and buildings, art and architecture all along this walk as if he could fill me up with his knowledge in one visit. "That's a ceiba, like in *El principito*."

"*The Little Prince*?"

"Yes, the tree. Your mother loved that."

"Oh, the baobab," I said, suddenly recognizing the tree that the Little Prince feared would overtake his tiny planet. The Little Prince carefully weeded his planet of the tiniest saplings because if not checked when they were small, the baobabs would grow and become dangerous, could disrupt the delicate balance of his world.

"Nance and I used to read *El principito* together," he said.

There was a dog-eared copy next to the fireplace at my grandparents' cabin, one that she had pulled off the shelves many times when I was young. She and my grandfather both loved the drawing of an elephant that had been eaten by a boa constrictor. The adults think it's a hat until the Little Prince sees the drawing and knows right away that it is an elephant inside a snake. I didn't tell my father that I had given Dave a copy of the book. On the front page I had inscribed my favorite quotation, the one I thought most romantic: "*You will be unique to me in all the world.*"

Wiggling my toes inside my new sandals, sitting beside my father beneath a baobab, I realized the gnarled roots were just as confused and twisted as our family tree, and even though I didn't know then how complicated, I knew the complexity was part of what made the tree beautiful.

As Sylvia began to walk on her little tamales, the world opened up to us. Now that I had left the hardships of her infancy behind, we began to explore the city in a new way. We ventured down the sidewalk that had just emerged from melting snow. I followed her around art museums as she walked on stocky legs. I brought her to the Minnesota Zoo, where she flapped her arms and waddled like the mandarin ducks and exotic poultry she saw there. My mother brought me to this same zoo when I was a child, and I felt a sort of symmetry to my own trips there. Like ghosts of myself and my mother, Sylvia and I explored the tropical exhibits and looked for the dolphins, which sprang from their tanks, and the gibbons, who swung from branch to branch on long arms. I pointed out these things to my daughter. "Look at the blue bird!" I said. "Can you see the big fish?" Sylvia stopped walking (not yet able to do two things at once) and looked, her big eyes taking in the scene.

My mother used to stop and stare patiently, waiting patiently for an animal to gain confidence and make an appearance. "Look! There's the wolf," she would exclaim upon spotting the creature. She would bend down to my level, pointing out the thick gray fur slinking through the pseudo-Alaskan tundra. Watching for a glimpse of a sleek coat or bushy tail, I learned to observe and wait: if you looked close enough and were quiet enough, you might find something hidden, something precious and fleeting.

In Cali, my father had also brought me to the zoo as if I were, even at twenty-one, a child who must be entertained. He and I had walked along sidewalks that wound their way through wooded exhibits and clapboard fences surrounding the lions and leopards, which paced the bare floors with bored indifference. Since I was an adult and not an excited five year old, I had found the families of the Colombians around me as captivating as the animals. I watched these prides and flocks and herds, the small children whose sticky hands were gripped by anxious parents, the teenagers who demanded money for sweets. At one exhibit a white-tailed deer stood under a eucalyptus. Her appearance had been such a funny surprise. In Minnesota, the species is found in every forest and park and suburban neighborhood. In the northern boreal forests, they nibble on dogwood and sumac, leave trodden paths along streams and lakes, where they splay their legs to drink fresh water. On twilit summer evenings, their white tails disappear into the purple light of dusk as they bound and leap through ferns and underbrush. But the doe in the Cali Zoo had stood motionless in her patch of dirt and chewed a twig as I watched. She didn't even bother to shake away the flies that landed on her ears and nose. Her brown fur was matted and damp; she looked trapped and sad.

I thought of the doe as I knelt beside my toddler. Sylvia peered through a mesh fence, trying to spot the macaw in the tropical bird exhibit. "Duck," she said, her label for all creatures with wings.

Through the cracks of the tropical soundtrack, I head the distinctive songs of native Minnesota sparrows and swallows rise and fall. The sparrows, I assumed, must have entered the zoo through an open window or doors left unintentionally ajar. Were they, then, as trapped as that doe in Cali had been? I listened to them as Sylvia paced around imitating the funny walk of the waterfowl. No, I supposed as I gathered her back into the stroller for the trek to the parking lot, these tiny birds were the brave ones, the strong ones, the ones who had charted their own course, the ones who came and went as they chose.

My father's voice, usually playful and cheery through the distorted phone line, was low and serious. Sylvia ran into the kitchen, where I held the phone in the crook of my neck. She was five now and full of energy, exhausting in a way so different from that of babyhood. We had somehow escaped the whirlwind of toddlerhood and shot straight into childhood. I shushed her as I strained to hear my father's words. "Anika, you need to call Silas," he said. "Beth is very sick. Silas is very upset. You need to call your brother."

For anyone with siblings, this directive is not unfamiliar, this command from a parent to do something for the sibling. But I wasn't sure I was someone with a sibling, not really. I had known about Silas for ten years now, but even after all this time I still used the words "my brother" like a wrist splint you might wear to prove you have an injury. I proclaimed the relationship in words and stories, but I didn't really feel it. In much the same way as I spoke of "my father," these labels felt false, unearned. When Dave and I first got married, I used every opportunity to say the words "my husband." *My husband and I are going out of town. My husband bought a new car. My husband went to the grocery store.* And every time I said it, I felt the thrill of the reality of the relationship, our connection, now legalized and verified. But that had not happened with Silas. No matter how many times I referred to him as my brother, it still felt false. Maybe I just didn't believe in it enough.

When I called Silas as directed, he told me, "My mom is really sick."

There was a flatness in his voice, a sound in the silences between his words that made my eyes sting. Selfishly, I thought of my own mother, who was, as she always claimed, "healthy as a horse." I murmured my sympathy, unsure what I should or could say.

There had been complications from Beth's lupus. Silas was with her at the hospital and had been there every day, Milenka home with their son.

"But we think she'll come home soon," he said, forcing optimism like air into a balloon.

I called him again a week or so later.

"They might have to amputate her foot," he said, his voice cracking as if the words choked him. I tried to imagine the Beth I had met—the woman who was solid and strong and no-nonsense, the woman who might have seduced my father but had also befriended my mother, lying in a hospital bed like the one Dave's mother had been in. I pictured the nurses and whiteboards, the scribbles that defined the ailments, the palliatives, the hope.

"I don't know what to do," Silas said. "What would she want?"

I couldn't answer. No one could. I didn't understand what was going on medically, and neither did anyone else. She had gotten so sick so fast that there was hardly time to think or act. I was worried about the medical care she was receiving.

My mother had told me that my surgery was one of the reasons she could never regret leaving Colombia. "If you would have had those problems there," she had told me once, "you might not have survived."

"I'm trying to get Renzo to come here," Silas said. As his mother sank deeper into sedation and oblivion, he became desperate for someone to help him. And he thought his father could be that for him. And when he talked of that plan, I couldn't decide if Silas would want me there, a sister but not really. Maybe my role was also nothing more than words strung together. The plan (or fantasy) of our father coming to the United States fell through.

By then, it was too late anyway. Beth died very suddenly with no decision needed on the amputation. She was less than ten years older than my mother, the only parent to two sons, one grandson. Silas's son was six when Beth died and couldn't understand why he couldn't see his grandmother. I cried for Silas. For Beth. For what would never be.

This life and death cycle, it was bullshit. Births and deaths as if in some kind of juxtaposition, some goddamn yin and yang of life. We want to be with family that are gone; we miss those we'll never see again; we confuse the ones we only think we know.

Beth's death seemed to rupture the tenuous bonds between my brother and me. Silas, a boy who had been disappointed and abandoned before, could see the loss only as the huge, infinite hole it felt like. And that made him, for a time, lost to me as well. His story isn't mine to tell, but he looked for solace in bars and alcohol, practiced the fine art of shots and tolerance, forgot things for the sole purpose of forgetting, and fought his demons with more demons. When Dave's mom had died, he had turned to me and searched for ways to appreciate life and see it through her eyes. I couldn't presume to do the same for my brother because, of course (and this became painfully clear all of a sudden), I barely knew him. His bereavement was deep and dark, and in many ways it scared me because I knew it could happen to me as well.

And so when, as he slowly climbed out of the abyss into which he had fallen, he suggested all of us (brother, sister, spouses, grandchildren) go to Colombia at Christmas, I said yes. Yes, we want to go to Colombia. Again.

28

ONCE WE WERE IN THE AIR over the Caribbean, it felt like a very bad idea. Our flight in Miami had been delayed, and the three of us, crammed into a row of seats on the port side of the aircraft, were exhausted. Sylvia would miss a few days of kindergarten before Christmas vacation, and I had left my mother with instructions to fill her stocking that hung by the fireplace. Our suitcases were filled with gifts (maple syrup for my father, earrings for Ceci, a Lego set for Santino) and warm weather clothes (short-sleeved shirts and sandals to be worn near the equator).

Silas and his family would already be in Popayán by the time we arrived. I had made most of the arrangements without actually talking to my father. It wasn't that I didn't want to speak to him, but I let Silas make all the phone calls and decisions, exchange emails about dates and times. I rationalized my lack of participation by letting myself believe that this was best for Silas, that it would help him heal after his mother's death. He wanted a father more than he wanted to be resentful.

But I was still wary of my father. And I was still reeling from having made this choice. It was enough that I had agreed to this reunion, enough that I had deigned to travel that distance, enough that I was willing to bring my child to Colombia. And when I imagined my daughter there, I couldn't stop myself from imagining all the dangers. Flight 965. The young men mistaken for military. The roadblock. The boy who pulled a pin out of a grenade.

Ceci's sister, María Elena, had told me that story when I stayed in Cali with my father. María Elena looked nothing like Ceci, had none of Ceci's vigor or wanderlust. She wore narrow skirts and slim-cut pants and kept her straight brown hair out of her face with a barrette. While Ceci was brown, María Elena was light, almost fair. And María Elena was a mother, looked after her children. And a tortoise.

"I teach special education for the blind," María Elena had told me, sitting back on her heels. She told me this as she fed the tortoise bits of frozen meat. "I have one student who makes it all worth it. He was just a toddler when he was playing in a mine field. Only," she paused, absently holding the next mouthful just out of reach of the tortoise, who strained with his prehistoric jaw, "he didn't know it was a mine field, of course. But he was just little, a little boy, and he saw a grenade. Only he didn't know it was a grenade, of course." I remember so clearly María Elena standing up and wiping her hands on a towel she had slung over her shoulder. She told me that he had picked up the grenade and pulled the pin out. "You know how children are."

I remember looking away from María Elena and watching the tortoise, who seemed to study her with his black eyes as if he, too, were listening to the story. Because that's all it felt like. A story. Something I would later retell when trying to explain what Colombia is. Twenty thousand deaths. What does that mean? Kidnappings. So abstract.

"He wasn't killed, but he was blinded by the grenade. And he lost both his hands." María Elena held up her hands as if they were useless. "The doctors split apart the two bones in his lower arms so now he can use them as pinchers." She moved the fingers of both hands open and shut to demonstrate. "He's almost completely independent now."

I didn't find out until much later how independent the boy was. I learned that he had finished high school in Colombia and gone to college in the United States. An Ivy League school, perhaps Harvard. A boy with no hands and no sight, a victim of time and place and circumstance. The story of this boy ached to show me that we don't have to be victims. But I couldn't let go of the fear.

I pictured the shaft of sunlight that shone through the blinds in María Elena's son's room. The light had aligned with the flat rock in the middle of the tortoise's pen as the creature climbed aboard with slow, precise movements, its claws scraping the surface with a clicking sound. With all the lessons I could have learned, this was the part I remembered. The ordinariness of a child in Colombia with a pet tortoise. This was what I had forced myself to think of, to hold on to with an iron-like clasp.

While I was desperately believing in hope and the ordinary, the whole plane dropped ten feet. Around us, there was a collective intake of breath as every passenger gasped in unison. We craned to look out the windows, although I'm not sure what we thought we would see. Outside the aircraft all that was visible were clouds and the reflection of the wings' navigation lights. The plane jerked again, and Sylvia, seated between us, was as wide awake as we were. She sat more upright in her seat, her waist straining at the seatbelt.

"Oh!" shrieked the people in the cabin as the plane bounced again and rattled side to side. I gripped the armrest with one hand, and Dave reached across Sylvia's lap to hold my other.

"Santa María, Madre de Dios, ruega por nosotros, pecadores," a man in the row behind us began chanting. "Dios te salve, María."

I looked back and saw him clutching a rosary, eyes closed, swaying back and forth in his seat.

The plane dropped again, and yet the cabin remained seated, no flight attendants appeared, no voice was heard on the loudspeaker.

"I didn't sign up for a roller coaster ride!" Sylvia said, now clinging to both our hands.

I tried to laugh. "It's pretty crazy, isn't it?" I said, but I felt sick.

A baby started to cry, and behind me a woman said in Spanish, "Babies know when something is wrong."

I looked at Dave and Sylvia. They could hear the praying, but they couldn't understand it, and I was thankful for that.

"Santa María, Madre de Dios," the man repeated. The woman seated next to him had begun praying with him, their voices rising in panic every time the plane rocked. "Dios te salve."

"Señoras y señores, we're going to try to move above the turbulence," the pilot finally announced just as passengers began locating the motion sickness bags tucked into seat pockets. "Things should calm down pretty soon."

I thought of my father and my brother waiting for us in Colombia. I thought of my mother at home filling Sylvia's Christmas stocking with trinkets and candy. The plane rocked violently again, first to one side, then the other. I felt like I was in an earthquake in California, like gravity and fear could not save me now.

Dave looked at me over Sylvia's head. "It's going to be okay," he said. And I had no choice but to believe him.

"Where's your Colombian passport?" the official asked in Spanish when we finally touched down, shaken but in one piece.

We had made it through both legs of our flight and had survived the worst air turbulence I had ever experienced, and now I felt in charge and in control. All of my anxieties had, for a time at least, dissipated. The relief at being on the ground gave me courage, a sense, however momentary, of invincibility. We might have fears, but we had taken all possible precautions, from bringing antibiotics in little orange canisters to carrying all our documents together.

I approached the immigration officer with confidence as Dave stood behind me gripping Sylvia's hand. She was wearing a pale peach dress covered in ruffles, and her brown hair was recently rebraided into two plaits. Dave's job was to carry the shoulder bag and wheel our suitcases. I was the translator, the expert. I was the Colombian. But without a Colombian passport.

I slid the three little blue books under the gap, where a brown hand grabbed them and opened each one to its page with our pictures. Sylvia's passport was shiny new with her gapped smile peering out of its pages (her teeth had since grown in). Dave's identification pictures are always more neck than face because the camera has to point upward to capture him. Mine, with something of a mug shot quality about it, was as unflattering as always.

But now the officer spoke in Spanish through the little round hole in the Plexiglas. "It says you were born in Colombia," he said, and I wondered if the glass was bulletproof. "Where is your Colombian passport?"

"No lo tengo."

When I was born, I was issued a Colombian certificate that listed place of birth (Popayán) and parents (Renzo and Nancy). At eighteen months, I was issued a certificate of birth abroad, a fancy affair with red ribbons and signed by Warren Christopher, the acting secretary of state (which my grandfather always thought was very impressive). This was my proof of existence: two birth certificates that declared me to be me. When my parents brought me to the United States just before my mother asked for a divorce, I had been a footnote to her U.S. passport. A little square black and white photograph of a screaming infant stapled into the pages was all that marked me as hers.

"You need a Colombian passport."

I didn't know this at the time, but Colombia had altered its constitution in 1991 to institute dual citizenship. A Colombian is a Colombian. Beginning during the liberal presidency of César Gaviria, anyone born in Colombia retains Colombian citizenship and qualifies for a national ID card and passport.

I pointed at my U.S. passport and clarified in my rusty Spanish that I was born in Colombia but raised in the United States, that my mother was American, that I was American.

"You were born in Colombia," he said, shaking his head. "You're Colombian." I thought of Silas passing through this same entry point, but with an American birthplace listed on his passport, encountering none of this confusion. I felt something that might have been sibling jealousy, and the sensation was both startling and strangely comforting.

"No." I tried to explain, "I have a U.S. passport." But with each badly pronounced word, my confidence drained away. The adrenaline that had kept me going since the flight seemed to be fading. I knew I was confusing verb tenses, and I couldn't remember the vocabulary I needed to describe myself. But what was I? This seemingly simple question was as complex as the one the man across the aisle had asked nearly fifteen years ago: *Are you visiting family?* The world seemed to want me to pick one side of the line or the other, but people—families—don't fit into neat columns. Family members could be strangers; I was an only child, and I had a brother; I was both Colombian and American. This was true.

"Then where are your naturalization papers?" the man asked.

"I'm not naturalized."

"Then you need a Colombian passport."

We were swirling around in a vortex of facts and data, each one a contradiction to another. I thought of the singer Shakira's first Spanish-language hit, a song María Fernanda and I had listened to over and over on the stereo in my father's studio when we were in our early twenties, practicing the lyrics that came loud and fast, a torrent of words. "*Here I am, loving you, drowning among the photographs and notebooks, among the things and mementoes that I don't understand . . .*" Singing with my Colombian cousin, I had looked around at the things in my father's studio—the tubes of paint, the half-filled canvases, the cardboard mailers, the photos on his desk, the souvenirs of his past. All this proof of everything that I didn't know and didn't understand. All those things hadn't made anything any clearer, hadn't prepared me for the secret of my brother. What use, I wondered, were the documents, the birth certificates, the passports, if they didn't tell the whole story?

"I don't have a Colombian passport," I said again.

The man behind the glass shook his head, then he held up his index finger, the universal signal to wait. "Momento."

When he left his little booth, it seemed the final omen against this whole trip. I shouldn't be here, this delay seemed to announce. Red tape and bureaucracy seemed to mean that I might never leave this spot. Would they make me board a plane again (more turbulence?) and send me back to my country even though *this* was my country?

I thought of the day my mother had decided to take me away. What if her plans had been foiled? What if she hadn't been able to take me away? I imagined a scene like a movie reel, the running, escaping, a mother carrying a wailing child in her arms, desperate to be free.

"Mommy," Sylvia called to me. And it wasn't just me now. She looked exhausted, her face pale and her brow wrinkled. The Spanish that surrounded her seemed to strip her of energy, and it made me wonder what it had been like for me coming to Minnesota as a baby, that crush of foreign sounds against my ear.

"Mommy's busy," Dave said. I could see fear and worry cloud his face. He was used to being the one to smooth the way for me and now for our daughter. And I could see the helplessness in his eyes. He took Sylvia's hand while I turned back to the empty booth.

It had been so easy before. Nearly fifteen years earlier, the man across the aisle had escorted me through the lines of first immigration and then customs. He had translated for both me and the agents, not only for language but also for nuance. He seemed to understand that I needed watching over. And now I was on my own, as adult as I could possibly be, feeling the pinch of responsibility in my stomach, my head. I wanted to cry, not only because of the frustration and fear but also because I wasn't sure I was ready for all this. Especially not if it was going to be this hard. I had thought receiving that email from my father had been a shock, but this reality of uniformed men and an upset, jet-lagged child seemed worse than any family secret.

At last the man returned to his booth and settled himself on his stool before picking up my passport again. "Bueno," he said as he explained something about dates and changes in laws. I barely listened much less understood, just felt grateful relief as he stamped first my American passport, then Dave's, then Sylvia's.

And before I was quite ready, we were through, walking down a white corridor toward Colombian soil once again, soil that suddenly felt safe and comforting.

29

MY FATHER'S HOUSE IN CAMPO BELLO looked almost identical to how I remembered it. The interior courtyard off the dining room still bloomed with impatiens and hibiscus, and the yellow canaries still feasted on mango pits. The same paintings still hung on the walls, and the same wooden ducks still swam across the glass coffee table in the living room.

During my first visit, my father had pointed out one of the ducks on the coffee table. It was smaller than my mallard with less detail to the finish. Black either by design or age, its feathers were indistinct, and its white beak had yellowed with the passing of years. The wooden toys he had manufactured in a *fábrica* in Silvia were eventually discontinued because of the lead paints used, but before all that the ducks were sold to art collectors around the world. For some reason, German collectors were particularly fond of these accurate replicas of the real things. I have a photograph from that era (probably sent to me in one of his enigmatic letters during my childhood) in which my father stands in a large room, presumably the factory's floor, rows of ducks lined up on the wide shelves behind him. "See this?" he had asked, pointing to small scratching along the edge of the body, little discolorations, barely discernible. "Those are your teeth marks."

Looking at the little scratches in the wood, I could almost feel the urge to masticate with my tiny nubs as if this physical confirmation of my existence in Colombia made my infancy come flooding back in a wave of nostalgia and imagined memories. Like the memory of the fountain, this was further evidence that I had lived and breathed and teethed here in this country of which I had no memory. If I had stayed, if I had grown up here, how many more objects, I wondered, would bear the evidence of my childhood?

"There is so much I want to tell," my father had said then. But he said nothing, nothing more. Instead of elaborating, instead of telling me, he had gone into the kitchen. I imagine now the weight of his knowledge—at least, I like to believe his secret weighed on him—and his agony over hiding it from me. I wonder if he debated whether to tell me while he opened the refrigerator and took out a bottle of Club Colombia. Perhaps he stood in the white and black kitchen, leaned on the red tile countertops, and considered telling me: "You don't know this, but you have a brother." Perhaps he rehearsed those words aloud while the sounds of the maid's television in her room garbled and snippets of conversation from outside slipped over the courtyard walls and into the house. But perhaps he heard all these sounds, and they mixed with the words in his head, and instead of saying anything he pried off the cap of his beer and returned to his daughter, who waited in the living room in front of the wooden ducks.

"Colombia is so fucking complicated," he had said, sitting on the couch next to me and swigging from the bottle. "It's a dangerous place. Everyone's fighting each other." He took another swallow before continuing. "There's the paramilitary, the drug cartels, the government, the guerrillas. You know how bad it is?"

I didn't say anything. I knew it couldn't be good, because Colombia at that time had been classified as the most dangerous country by the U.S. State Department. In 1995 alone there had been twenty-five thousand murders, many at the hands of the warring FARC. Kidnappings, a tool used to broker power and make money, were on the rise, and paramilitaries, in an attempt to stem their influence, massacred entire villages thought to be sympathetic. But during that trip I had been sheltered more or less from the national conflict. On the other hand, I had felt perpetually afraid—although that might not have had anything to do with the place.

"Listen: it all started out ideological. You know, they were fighting for Marxism and communism and shit. But now everyone is corrupt and just wants to get rich. It's all about fucking money."

Colombia's civil war has been in progress since 1958, and there was unrest even before that, bombings my mother had witnessed and yet had paid no attention to. Like my parents' marriage, Colombia's embrace of communism and socialism had been a good idea in theory. The left-wing guerrillas, groups like FARC and the ELN, had originally been formed by Communists and liberals who had been influenced by Che Guevara (whom my mother, she had told me, had found handsome and dashing back then) and by Cuba's revolution and by the Cold War. It had been born out of poverty and frustration, inequality and inattention. Revolution so often gets tainted by the idealism of ideologies.

"This damn war just keeps going on," my father said, his words slurring slightly, his accent more pronounced by the influence of alcohol.

At the time, I had just listened, stunned into silence by these complex political revelations. I claimed myself as a Colombian, but I knew nothing about Colombian history or its struggles, nothing, really, about its culture or past. Now I try to imagine what it would be like to watch something you love be destroyed by itself. I wonder about all the loss my father must have seen from the disarray of his country to the dissolution of his marriage. He had felt betrayed, and perhaps his secret-keeping had been a reaction to that sense of betrayal.

"No one knows when the fuck to stop," he said, setting down the empty bottle.

The living room was quiet, and the only light came from the dining room. I studied the gnawed duck on the table.

"Colombia is so beautiful," he said. "I want you to see how beautiful it is, my dear Anika."

He went to the kitchen again and came back with another bottle. "Lots of things went wrong," he said. "Next time, there is so much I want to tell you."

But there hadn't been a next time, not until now.

And now I already knew what he had wanted to tell me. At least,

I assumed that was what it had been. As he and Ceci watched Sylvia run from room to room exploring the house, I couldn't tell if he was thinking of my last visit or if he had already moved on, ready to be a grandfather. Sylvia ran to the Christmas tree they had set up in the living room and then bounded down into the courtyard, relishing the feeling of fresh air on her bare legs.

"It's summer!" she shouted joyously, as incongruous as the crepes had been the night of my arrival so long ago.

On the afternoon of that first day in Popayán, Sylvia and I collapsed in the bedroom, the room that had been mine, its walls still painted golden yellow. Ceci's maid had served us *sancocho*, a traditional chicken stew from the region.

"I know you like *tajadas*," Ceci had said to Silas, presenting him with a platter of fried sweet plantains. I felt a litany of jealousies wash over me—that she knew that about him, that he knew what *tajadas* were, that my brother was receiving an attention that I wasn't. But my jealousy was short-lived because there, too, were the chunks of mango and papaya and *piña* that I loved.

"Mangos for you, Anika," Ceci had said, beaming.

I bit into a fresh Colombian mango and felt the rush of recognition wash over me. The first time that I had tasted mango as an adult had been in my mother's kitchen. I was home from college, and she had bought me a fresh mango from the supermarket, one of those half-red, half-green things one gets in Minnesota. She had sliced it into misshapen chunks, and we had stood in the kitchen of her little house. That day, the taste of the soft, sugary flesh had bombarded me with a distinct feeling of home, albeit a distant, ethereal home, nothing more than a sensation, void of specifics. The mango was honey sweet, and it inexplicably made me want to cry.

My mother had watched me. "You used to teethe on mango seeds in Colombia. I used to cut them up and give you the seed. You just held on to it with your chubby little hands and gnawed on it."

I ate the juicy slices and stared at her, suddenly feeling that if I had teethed on mango seeds as a baby, who was this person in Minnesota? If I had grown up in the Midwest, who was the child that tasted tropical fruits? That I had teethed on mango seeds made me wonder if I had parallel lives—two roads and one not taken.

"Haven't I ever told you that before?" my mother had asked then.

There were so many things that she didn't know she needed to tell me. Tasting the mango for the first time in my mother's kitchen had overwhelmed me with sweetness and safety, a sort of déjà vu. I didn't remember the mango seeds from my infancy, but there was, stored somewhere in my hippocampus, a recollection of orange-yellow flesh and strands of pulp.

"¿Quieres mango?" Ceci asked Sylvia, who had so far refused the soup, rice, and fresh-squeezed juice. Sylvia was overwhelmed with the sights and smells, the sound of her own mother speaking in a foreign tongue. She was exhausted and confused with culture shock and something more deeply felt, I think—that sense of the known being suddenly unknown.

After lunch Sylvia and I walked like zombies into the bedroom, while my father poured shots of *aguardiente* for Silas and Dave. My husband towered over the two Colombian men by at least a foot, and his skin appeared especially pale in the light of the house. But he was filled with something like elation, perhaps from the plethora of flowers or the mountain air or maybe simply the chance to see this land from which his wife originated. Dave had been warned about the strong, anise-flavored sugar-cane liquor, but as I closed the bedroom door, I could hear him clinking glasses with my father and my brother.

30

THE SLEEP OF THE JET-LAGGED can be disturbingly deep, especially in the late afternoon. I awoke in the yellow light of the bedroom to find that Sylvia had gotten up, probably to play with her cousin. I lay in bed with my eyes closed, picturing the courtyard outside the French doors of the bedroom, the dandelion yellow of the walls. I remembered the vase of gerbera daisies that had greeted me in this room, the one they had called "my bedroom." I sniffed the air, but there were no flowers this time.

From beyond the closed door, I heard the high-pitched laughter of the two six-year-olds playing in the other room. Santino had introduced Sylvia to video games, and I could envision the two staring at his tablet, their heads together. Except for his mop of curly dark-blond hair passed down to him from Beth, Santino looked just like his father. And Sylvia looked just like me except for her fair coloring; her eyes are hazel, just like my mother's. Before this trip, we had visited my brother for short, sometimes awkwardly forced vacations in California several times, so we already knew that Santino is shorter but faster than his cousin. We had already seen that although Sylvia's vocabulary often confused Santino, he talked more (and louder) than she did. Even though they hadn't seen each other in more than a year, they were already conspiring together in my father's house like it was their own, two only children ignoring the adults as much as possible.

I shut my eyes again and listened to the clink of glasses from the dining room. My body felt the heavy weight of jet lag. My legs were boulders, my arms fallen logs. My head was fuzzy as if I were the one drinking shots. I kicked off the sheet and listened to the sounds of the men talking from across the courtyard, their voices carrying as if they were in the room with me.

"She's not mad at you," I heard Silas say.

"She won't forgive me."

It was my father's voice, and my heart beat in time to the canaries' chattering at the courtyard bird feeder. I opened my eyes, squinting against the yellow light.

"Listen," my father said, his consonants blurred by alcohol. "Listen, you can be in love with two women at the same time."

Silas made a sound like agreement.

"I loved your mom," my father said to Silas. A bottle clinked again. Must have been a refill, another shot, more clear liquid. "You have to believe that." Louder.

"I do."

"I loved your mom." More clinking. "And I loved Nancy, too."

What did he know of love, I thought. I thought of Dave's hand on mine after I fell off the bicycle, of my mother taking care of the baby when I was at my most fragile, of Silas needing to talk to me when his mother was sick. I thought of my father's sporadic emails and rare phone calls, of his paintings that he seemed to think could stand in for something.

"You can love two women at once."

I sat up.

Love the One You're With.

A wave of nausea swept over me like an earthquake. It wouldn't have been the first time I had vomited in his house. I lay down again, and the sensation passed.

My father's voice again. With hard edges like the corner of a building, a wall. "But she won't forgive me."

He was talking about me. Even with my eyes closed, tears leaked out onto the pillow. I thought of those gerbera daisies. The Colombian flowers, he had told me, that were shipped to Paris each day to be sold at flower markets. But my father had never been to Paris, much less Europe. He could talk about these places—places like Paris and

Minnesota—but they were not really part of his life, they were his imagined fantasies. Through my closed lids, I could see the light of the room, and the air itself felt suffocating.

"She was just surprised," I heard Dave say, entering the discussion, defending me. His voice was steady, calm. The only clue that he was drunk this afternoon was the unusual volume.

"But why should she be?" my father said, making a noise like a snort or maybe a cough. "She had to know." I could picture him pointing a brown finger at Dave as if by gesture he could convince someone. "Shit. I knew she would be mad. This is why I didn't tell her."

"Just think how she felt," Silas said. "You kept a pretty big secret."

I heard the sound of a bottle on glass. I was crying now, listening to these ideas my father had about me. My body heaved in silent sobs, and I sat up in bed, then stood up.

"After I told her, she stopped talking to me. She wouldn't fucking talk to me."

"Give her time." Silas's voice was calm and, like Dave's, louder than usual.

"She hasn't forgiven me."

If I had not forgiven him, I wouldn't have come. I had told him once that he swore too much, and he had laughed at me. "Oh, come on," he had said in his accent that attacked the vowels, "you don't care."

"You sound like you're left over from the sixties," I had told him, not realizing at the time that this might be insulting, that perhaps he thought himself a hip and modern man.

"Shit," he had said.

It wasn't that I was a prude, it wasn't that curse words bothered me, it was that it didn't feel like he was my father if he swore in front of me. And I wanted him to be my father. I did.

I walked to the door and then changed my mind. I climbed back into bed, turned away from the window. How could he be my father if he didn't understand me? I wondered. How could we ever build these bonds? I felt an ocean of regret that I had come here at all. Suddenly I was frightened—more frightened than I had been on the flight after the plane crash, more frightened than I had been on that mountain road in front of the machine guns. I was frightened because I didn't know if this could be repaired and if I could be a Colombian daughter. Our return flight was in ten days, and those hours and minutes stretched before me like an eternity.

31

CECI'S SILVER SUZUKI was more than twenty years old now and had been confined to the garage for storage, so for our visit she had borrowed a little SUV for our trip to Silvia. I wondered if perhaps she held on to that car the way my father had clung to the yellow baby carrier, these mementos from the past that feel like proof of who we are. For my father, the carrier proved that he was a father; for Ceci, the Suzuki proved she was an adventurer. The things we keep around us are powerful talismans.

Above the fireplace in our Minneapolis house, in a place of prominence, I display a painting by my father. He had sent it to me when I was in college, just a few months after my visit. It had arrived rolled in a tube plastered with airmail and customs stickers, and I had to bring it to a framing shop to get it stretched.

"I need to have this stretched," I had said, laying it on the counter and waiting for someone to remark on the beauty and poignancy of the painting, waiting to be asked who the artist was. I had longed to say aloud: *my father.* The painting depicted a night scene with dark-blue skies and rolling green-black hills. White swirls made the moon, and pinpricks of paint were the stars. Already Colombia felt like something that hadn't happened, but here it was, captured in the way my father could capture reality and remembrance in line and tint. It had arrived with a note written in my father's block script: *Recording the Stars,* he called it.

I had immediately known the significance of this scene. We had gone to see a movie in Cali: *Il Postino,* an Italian film with Spanish subtitles. The film told the story of the poet Pablo Neruda's 1952 exile from Chile and his time in Italy. In the film, Neruda helps a young man win over a beautiful woman through poetry, like Cyrano and Christian before them. Watching the story unfold, I had thought about my parents, about what had brought them together, what brought anyone together in that almost violent emotion of love. In the movie theater in Cali, my father and I had watched the woman finally fall into the arms of the young man, won over by poetry, by beauty. At the end of the film, when Neruda leaves the country, the young man wants his idol to remember him and Italy. He records the sounds of his country—the fishing boats, the busy café. "I am recording the stars at night," the Italian man said in the movie, holding a microphone up to the night sky.

Recording the Stars. Holding the note in my hand, I had remembered the stars, the sound of the night air in Cali. And I had remembered my father's deep, almost childlike laugh. And I thought about love stories and about how they aren't always what you expect them to be. The film was, like my father's, a love story about art. He had been an artist from the earliest age, had always looked at the world through a lens of color and line. And to his art he had been true—more true than he had been to my mother, to me.

"What kind of frame were you thinking?" the salesperson had asked. And I knew that I would not be explaining to this stranger that I had a Colombian father, that I was born there, that I was a fascinating and special person.

The road to Silvia was no better than I remembered it with its steep drop-offs and potholed asphalt, but I was grateful we weren't bouncing around in the Suzuki. Even so, the eight of us—two parents, two siblings, two spouses, and two grandchildren—were piled into the Hyundai Tucson, squeezed hip to hip. The luggage and food were in the back, and my father's spoiled dog sat on his lap.

I was in the front seat with Sylvia on my lap, thumb in her mouth. As Ceci maneuvered through a treacherous detour over nothing more than a dirt trail, she told me in Spanish that the rerouting was the result of the bombing of a bridge by guerrillas. This was a common occurrence, she told me, the guerrillas having sharpened their tools of war by concentrating on transit corridors and economic disruption more than kidnappings.

"What did she say?" asked Dave from his cramped spot in the back seat.

"Nothing," I said.

What he and Sylvia didn't know would keep them safe, I thought. But I couldn't hide from them the checkpoints at each town we passed through, the men who guarded the main streets with machine guns and crisp uniforms. I watched Sylvia watch them, wide eyed, and wondered if not explaining things made them even scarier. But she didn't ask, and I didn't tell her. Perhaps that was how my father had felt when he kept his own explanations secret. Perhaps he had thought he was protecting me, keeping me safe.

At last Ceci stopped the car in front of a white adobe building, and we all tumbled out like clowns. My father now kept a house in the center of Silvia. Built in the mid-eighteenth century as part of a compound belonging to wealthy Spanish settlers, the house was part of a building that took up an entire block of the town with its whitewashed walls and red tile roof. The original house had been subdivided into smaller homes and businesses.

My father unlocked a thick wooden door, so small Dave had to duck to enter. I stood watching the crowd across the street.

"Look," my father said, pointing. "Those are all the wives bailing their husbands out of jail."

I laughed and elbowed Dave. "He says those people are paying bail." My father liked to joke, liked to capitalize on his country's infamous reputation, liked to make Colombia sound more primitive and treacherous than it was. Then I noticed that painted on the building across the street was the word *Cárcel*. It *was* a jail. I laughed again as I stepped across the 250-year-old threshold.

The portion of the building that was my father's house had thick adobe walls and uneven stone floors. The white-painted ceilings were crisscrossed with thick beams as wide as a man's waist. My father lit a crackling fire in the hearth in one corner of the main room, and it struggled to warm the cavernous space. The back rooms of the house held his drafting table and paints, a spare bed, and stretched blank canvases awaiting inspiration. The courtyard included a dry cistern decorated with ceramic mosaic designs, and bunches of marigolds bloomed in the cold mountain air. Even though the adults thought it was chilly, Sylvia relished the feeling of walking the bricks in stocking feet and refused to wear a sweater as she skipped around and in the cistern. The house had a primitive kitchen with a hot plate and fireplace, and while Sylvia and Santino ran in and out of the rooms shouting and chasing one another, Ceci patched together a meal for us.

The two children ran and explored, and my father, who wasn't feeling well, retreated to his bedroom. The rest of us sat at the worn wooden table in the kitchen and kept warm by huddling shoulder to shoulder and toasting with one shot of *aguardiente* after another.

"Here's to being in Colombia finally!" I said. We clinked glasses.

"Here's to family," Silas said.

"Here's to aguardiente!"

"Here's to secret brothers!"

"And sisters!"

My brother and I sat on the bench against the wall that my father had painted bright blue and on which hung a framed 1970s poster from the Minneapolis College of Art and Design, where he had briefly been a student. As if being in Silvia wasn't surreal enough, this reminder of Minnesota stabbed the air with poignancy. Silas put his arm around me and squeezed, pulling me toward him. He smelled like anise and cigarettes and damp wool from the jacket he wore. Dave snapped a picture of us from across the table, one that turned out as blurry as we felt.

"Se acabó el aguardiente," Ceci said as she went to pour herself a drink from the empty bottle. "We can go get more."

After dinner my father agreed to stay with the kids while the rest of us went in search of more liquor. As we stumbled down the street, free from our children and our father, Silas threw his arm over my shoulder and said, "Let the grandpa babysit. He needs a taste of what it's like to actually have a kid."

After we bought a fresh bottle of the licorice-flavored liquor from the corner store (which came with a stack of plastic medicine cups in which to pour shots), we wandered to the plaza, where we sat on a bench drinking *tragos.* The plaza was illuminated with Christmas lights in purple, yellow, and bright pink, and a few people still loitered in the chilly night.

"Look." Dave pointed across the plaza. A motorcyclist and a small white car were stopped, and each driver was being questioned by soldiers dressed in dark uniforms and neat little hats. At least three men surrounded each vehicle, and all of them carried their machine guns with the barrels pointed at the ground. I looked around the plaza at a group of Guambiano Indians who sat in a close-knit circle, the empty bottle alone on the brick path. Leaning back, I looked up at the night sky, imagined all the things I could not see from this cheery spot. The treacherous mountain slopes, the hidden activities, more soldiers that were looking for something. People loitered outside a small pub, where a group of musicians played what Ceci told us was Christmas music. The horns were flat, and the drummer beat slightly out of rhythm, but the music filled the night air and crept into the mountains above us.

Silas put his arm over my shoulder again and, slurring his words, said again, "Let the grandpa babysit. He has no idea."

Earlier that day we had stopped at the *panadería* that faced this plaza, a little shop that sold the *pandebono,* little doughnut-shaped salty, cheesy breads. Ceci had ushered us in, calling out to the proprietors, "¿Qué hubo?"

She and my father knew the owners of the bakery, and a woman with short gray hair came out from behind the counter. "Don Renzo," she said, giving them both kisses on the cheeks. "Señora."

"These are Renzo's grandchildren," Ceci had explained, putting her hands on the heads of Sylvia and Santino, both of whom ducked away and grabbed the doughy treats out of the bag I held. "And this is Renzo's daughter."

The woman took my hand. "I remember your mother," she told me in Spanish. She held her hand out to indicate a large belly. "She was pregnant with you." She laughed. "So pregnant."

Silas was standing outside the shop, and I looked at him through the doorway. I wondered if this woman also remembered Beth. Had Beth bought her daily breads and sweets from this *panadería* when she stayed in Silvia with my father? And if she had, did this woman know the sordid story of my father's love affairs? I understood that in Colombia relationships and family could be complicated, that allowances were made for men with wandering eyes, and that any event that resulted in the birth of a child could be forgiven. Could my brother and I now forgive our father?

Silas downed another plastic medicine cup of *aguardiente*. "He needs to get a taste of what it's like to actually have kids. Every day. All the time."

I clinked cups with him, but what I wanted was to laugh with him, not talk about our father. "Look at her," I said, pointing at our father's wife, who, for some reason, was now wearing a headlamp that illuminated the night sky as she leaned back to finish her shot. Milenka had moved to the low wall that surrounded the plantings in the plaza and was walking along it like a child on a balance beam. Every time Ceci turned to look at her, Milenka was bathed in the spotlight from Ceci's head. Silas sighed for an instant, and then he laughed, too, at this scene. All of us began to laugh, the kind of laughter that you feel deep in your belly, in your heart, in your soul. We laughed until we wept tears of something that tasted of letting go. Dave set down his empty cup next to the half-full bottle of *aguardiente* and captured the scene in off-kilter photographs.

Silas scooped up the bottle and poured fresh shots for all of us. "¡Aguardiente!" he said, a sort of battle cry.

Later, as we walked crookedly home through the quiet streets of Silvia, Silas and I hung behind the others. He swirled the last swallow of clear liquid in his cup. "My mom was supposed to be on this trip. That was the plan. She wanted to come back, and we were all going to come here together. Now I'm going to scatter her ashes instead."

I knocked shoulders with him. He swiped away something in his eye and downed the fiery drink.

"Have some more." We stopped walking as he unscrewed the cap and poured me another cupful. "I kind of hope they don't behave."

At first, I wasn't sure what he was talking about, and then I realized he was referring to our children left to the care of their grandfather, who had never really been a father. Each of them only children as I had been, they were challenging in their own ways. Santino was addicted to his iPad and the games and movies loaded on it. He had little interest in books or art projects and so had to be cajoled to do other things. Meanwhile, Sylvia studied with interest the hand of her *abuelo* moving across paper but could be selfish and standoffish and shy. She was sensitive. Sensitive to all things: dogs, noisy cars, right and wrong.

When she was three years old, she had kicked me in the shin by accident with her little wild foot, and I told her (in the way parents have been saying for eons), "You need to say 'sorry' for kicking me."

But instead of apologizing, she had started to cry and through her tears had wailed, "But I didn't mean to!"

"But you hurt me," I said. "And when we hurt someone we say sorry, even if we didn't mean to."

I thought about that now, about how we are expected to apologize even when we never meant to injure the people we love. I thought of my father withholding the truth from me for so many years. I thought of his complaining the other day that I hadn't forgiven him. But how, I thought, could I forgive someone who hadn't said sorry?

In Spanish, to apologize is to say *lo siento*, which literally translated means "I feel it." My mother had gone through her life feeling everything, apologizing even when she wasn't to blame. As a nurse, she would apologize to her patients, the doctors, the other nurses. She apologized to my stepfather even when he treated her like a possession or a servant. She apologized to her parents even though they had often overlooked her as a child. My mother apologized to strangers standing in line at movie theaters, to repairmen making house calls, to veterinarians treating her cats. And she apologized to me, telling me how sorry she was that she had in some way not given me her idea of a perfect upbringing.

"I'm so sorry you had to go through all that," she told me. "I wish I could have protected you better."

But I knew that none of her choices were meant to harm and that the things that happened were not solely her fault. Now I think about how she and my father really shared the blame in the breakup of their marriage and complications of custody over me, their only child. Despite the fact that my mother did the unthinkable—to steal away a child from a father—she owned that choice. And because she apologized, there was nothing for me but to forgive her. To forgive her meant to accept my mother with all her flaws, to love her despite them and because of them. I knew that she felt what I was feeling, and this bound us together in a way that I longed for with my father. I desperately wanted to hear him say, "*lo siento.*" I feel it. I wanted him to admit his part, to acknowledge that he could feel the hurt he caused me. I wasn't sure if he didn't say it because he didn't want to feel it or because he couldn't.

"They probably won't behave," I said to Silas. "Those two will be wild and crazy, asking for treats and not going to bed." My brother laughed with me, and the *aguardiente* burned as it slid down my throat before coming to rest in my gut, heavy and harsh.

32

THE NEXT DAY, WEDNESDAY, was market day in Silvia, the traditions of this ancient village marching forward with no concern for our headaches and upset stomachs from the three bottles of *aguardiente* we had consumed. Our father was as energetic as his two grandchildren, who, unlike us, had slept last night. Despite rain that thundered on the plastic roof of the market building, he led the way through the sidewalks to the building.

Sylvia held tightly to my hand as we let Dave part the crowds ahead of us. Among the stalls, a stench like wet dog overpowered even the smell of cooking *arepas*. Shoppers jostled and bumped as they made their way through the tables laden with stacks of brown cakes of the sugar cane sweetener *panela*, piles of guavas as big as a child's head, row after row of sacks of potatoes and onions, mountains of yucca and plantains and cassava. Men in the Guambianos' traditional narrow, cobalt-blue skirts and bowler hats squinted at customers, while the women, wearing smiles riddled with gaps, clasped handfuls of money as they bartered and argued over prices and quality. My mother, despite being as shy and standoffish as her granddaughter, had told me that she grew to like the interactions with vendors. She liked the way, at the close of the transaction, the buyer and seller would exchange handshakes as if to say, *No matter how much I just fought you, I respect you.*

In addition to the food vendors, artists sold weavings and cotton bags called *mochilas* and adobe ceramics. Sylvia fingered little wooden turtles and clay figurines in the shape of horses and chickens. As she wavered over the choices, I remembered the first time my father had taken me to the *mercado* in Silvia, when I, too, had been unsure of what I should buy. I remember strolling the market aisles (which had been much less crowded then) with the unfamiliar pesos in my purse, nervous that I would choose the wrong keepsake, an inferior souvenir, an inartistic weaving. I had wanted to impress both him and this country, as if by purchasing the right gifts I could prove that I belonged and that I deserved to be half Colombian. I eventually chose a small weaving that depicted a traditional Guambiano family surrounding a campfire. At the time I had thought I would give it to my mother, but I ended up giving it to Dave, and for many years it hung above his bed, where I could glance up at it as we made love.

My father now caught up to us as we passed a woman holding a bundle to her breast that smelled of ripe diapers. He grabbed Sylvia's arm as a man stumbled into us, a bottle of *aguardiente* clutched in his hand. My father leaned toward me and whispered, "The Guambianos come here and spend all their money on aguardiente before they go back to their village." He laughed at their misfortune, and I felt my stomach turn at this. Once when I was about six or seven, my grandparents came across a print of an American Indian girl. The girl in the painting was about my age with a leather beaded dress and colorful headband. And she looked just like me. I could have been the model who sat for that portrait, the likeness was so striking. At the time, no one voiced the question that must have been in their minds. What blood ran through my veins? Was I descended from Indians? I had once asked my father, my father with his brown skin and wiry hair, if we had Indian or African blood. *No!* he had said, and I had let it go. One more thing I would never really know the answer to.

"You watch," he said. "Tonight you'll see them at the jail." He winked, and I left him as he paused to light a cigarette.

"What do you think, Sylvia?" Ceci asked in Spanish. She crouched down to my daughter's level, but Sylvia said nothing. "When it stops raining, we can ride horses." Sylvia just looked at her blankly, overwhelmed by the smells and sounds and chaos of the *mercado*.

When we arrived back at the house, Ceci tried again.

"Caballos," she said to Sylvia. She made horse sounds and gal-loped across the stone floors. But Sylvia declined to play this game of charades.

"Do you want to ride horses?" I finally interpreted.

"I do!" shouted Santino from the other room. Like his father, he always seemed ready for anything.

"Maybe," Sylvia said at last. Like me, she was careful, wary, and promised nothing, preferring instead to wait and see.

The horses were stabled in a low, whitewashed building along a dirt road. Bougainvillea almost obscured the sign that read *Se Aquilan Caballos.* My father paid for the horses, which would take us on a loop along the road, up the mountain, and back again. I put one foot in the stirrup and climbed awkwardly on the horse as the saddle creaked under my weight.

The last time I had been on a horse was at a *finca* outside Popayán. The ranch belonged to friends of Ceci, and we had been invited for a New Year's Day celebration. Palacé was like a film version of a Latin American plantation, with a big white house and a wraparound front porch, where crowds of people (relatives? friends?) had gathered. Inside the women congregated in the kitchen around piles of plantains, bloody chicken parts, and unshucked corn that were being prepared for the huge vats of *sancocho* they would make. Outside, my father had introduced me to my cousin Renzito, the first Fajardo grandson. Renzito (named after my father) was studying to be an electrical engineer, just like Dave.

"Ay, Anika," he said to me as we stood in the yard outside the house. Renzito was four years older than I was, old enough to remember me from when I was a baby, from before I left Colombia. He remembered the baby bottle I dragged around everywhere and the scowl I wore whenever dissatisfied. "We're so glad you're here. My tío Renzo is so happy."

I looked over at my father, who was talking with some of the other men and sat smoking cigarettes on the porch steps. It hadn't occurred to me that he was somebody's uncle. The family relationships, even then, had seemed so mysterious.

"Have you ever ridden a horse, Anika?" my cousin asked in Spanish.

"No, never."

"What?"

My father heard us and called to me from the porch. "Try. You like."

And before I knew what was happening, a huge and dappled gray horse was in front of me. My mother used to sing me a lullaby about all the pretty little horses, but this one was immense and smelled of musk and straw. I backed up a bit.

"Get on," my cousin urged.

"¡Espera! Wear this!" Ceci called. She had just emerged from the house and nabbed a panama hat off one of the men who sat smoking. "Cowgirl!" she said in English, laughing as she placed the hat on my head.

"Help her up," I heard someone say as a fly buzzed over the horse's gray coat. And then I felt a stranger's hand on my rear, and in a few awkward moments I was up on the animal, overlooking the relatives and the *finca*. From atop the horse, I remembered that I had seen pictures of a Colombian *finca* before in my mother's black and white photographs of her time there in 1969. She and Melinda had come to a *finca* with a couple of boys they had met during their first few months in Colombia, when they still put curlers in their hair and wore skirts. She had told me this with some embarrassment, saying that it was unheard of for girls to go unchaperoned with boys they had just met. Their visit with Fernando and Enrique—or was it Boris?—is immortalized in the snapshots of wide innocent smiles.

"There was a housekeeper," my mother had told me, "and she certainly didn't approve of us being there." They drank Coca-Cola chasers after the burning taste of *aguardiente,* and I suspect they inhaled the grassy smoke of marijuana, although she didn't admit to that.

From my perch on the gray horse on the grounds of the *finca*, I found myself in awe of my mother's daring; I felt unbalanced and dizzy. I was afraid of falling, of the horse, and maybe even of simply the new experience. I was, at that time, already older than my mother had been when she married my father. But I felt so uncertain.

But with Sylvia settled in front of me, gripping the saddle's horn with all her might, I felt more secure. As the horse began to move, its body heat radiating through my jeans and the motion of its breathing visible on its flanks, Sylvia squealed with something between shock and delight. That she was on this beast at all was something of a miracle for this sensitive child, but I suspected that the fact that her cousin rode with his mother, too, had helped spur her on.

"This is Princess," she said, confidently naming the horse and assigning it a gender.

The animal began its rote path toward the mountain trail, and Sylvia and I rocked with the motion.

"Whoa!" she shrieked. And then she laughed.

Princess plodded ahead, her bones shifting with each step.

"Oooh." Sylvia clung to the saddle, both exhilarated and terrified.

Silas and his horse galloped closer to us. "What do you think, Sylvia?" he asked his niece. Sylvia was his niece, I was Santino's aunt, and the two children were cousins. All these incredible relationships, all of us on horseback at eight-thousand-foot elevation.

Sylvia grinned. "Can we go faster?"

The horses were gentle and docile along a trail they had clearly taken dozens of times, each one following the other.

"I don't think we can make this horse do anything," I said. That New Year's Day at the *finca*, my cousin had taken hold of the bridle with a sure grip, and from the safety of the solid ground, asked, "Where do you want to ride?" Maybe I could have learned something up there, maybe I could have felt whatever it was that had made my mother smile in those days, maybe I could have faced my fears on that bright New Year's Day. Maybe if I had said yes, I would have discovered something that would have led to living a different life than I led. But instead, I had scowled like I had when I was a baby and said no. "I want to get down."

"Santino!" Sylvia yelled at her cousin, who was a few yards ahead of us on his mother's horse. "What's your horse's name?"

Santino turned to look at her and shook his head. "I don't know its name."

"Mine's name is Princess," Sylvia said confidently, letting go of the horn for a moment to stroke its white flank.

33

A FEW YEARS AFTER DAVE'S MOTHER DIED, we brought her ashes to a river in Minnesota that flows into Lake Superior. It was a warm summer day, but near the lake the temperature dropped, cooled by the great expanse of fresh water. My father-in-law poured a handful of dried rose petals into my palm from a ziplock bag, and I dropped the petals one by one into the water that ran golden with tannins. Then I stood back as the three men of my husband's family crouched on a rock and let the ashes cloud above the water and then dissipate into the crisp midwestern air.

Now I watched Silas do the same, his father and his son crouching beside him on a rock on a river high in the Colombian Andes. This *río* begins somewhere in the mountains as a tiny trickle that gains momentum as it tumbles downhill. Its waters run deep and wild, brown from the churning sediment. It goes by various names as it passes first through Silvia, then the town of Piendamó, and then Popayán before it makes its way to the Magdelena River. The same waters would eventually work their way north to the Caribbean, where its mountain water would mix with the sapphire blue of the sea.

When Ceci pulled the packed Hyundai to a stop along the riverbank, Silas grabbed the box containing his mother's ashes, and the rest of us followed him down a footpath. Beth had met our father in Silvia, and the two of them had spent time working along this river. It had been her desire to be brought back here, to this spot, this river, this memory.

As we walked down the path, we caught a glimpse of a contraption on a pulley, something like a Rube Goldberg invention, spanning the river. A wooden box about the size of a banana crate was suspended above the water by cables. A child in a brightly colored dress and bare feet was riding in it as another barefooted child pulled the ropes to bring her across the fifteen-foot chasm. She jumped out, and the two of them ran ahead and disappeared around a bend in the river. Our own American children watched this display of independence with some awe, while Dave and Ceci each observed the scene through the viewfinders of their cameras and snapped pictures of the vertical mountain slopes. As Silas and our father made their way down the slope to the water's edge, I pointed out to Sylvia the brown cow that grazed at a precarious angle on the grass.

From our spot above the river's edge, we watched Silas leap from the bank to a large boulder, Santino close behind him. The three generations of men crouched near the water. Silas opened a small box, and even though I couldn't see or hear from where we waited, I knew he was weeping. I remembered watching Dave and his dad letting the ashes go, knowing I couldn't help, couldn't change anything, couldn't make reality hurt any less. I looked away just as gray dust blew across the churning water, feeling far away from my brother, feeling like an interloper in his private moment, a moment he shared with this father we shared.

I was relieved when Sylvia tugged at my sleeve wanting a snack. Ceci opened the Hyundai's hatch, and Sylvia sat on the edge eating a granola bar and dangling her little tamales above the dirt road in Guambia above the town of Silvia. Soon Silas would dry his eyes, and we would all pile back into the car to rumble and rattle past makeshift huts, dozens of loose chickens, and a horse or two that lined the river's path toward home.

34

WHETHER FROM THE COLD AIR in Silvia or the horse ride or a virus caught from her cousin, who had been sick when he arrived, two days before Christmas Sylvia spiked a fever over 103, her little body limp and lethargic. We didn't know what it was, but I shifted from daughter and sister into parent mode. When your child is sick, you go into tunnel vision, put on blinders. You push aside fears of unnamed noises and imagined dangers. No matter how worn out and overwrought you are, you move forward. I couldn't be a daughter while my own lay quiet and still under thin blankets.

That night, in our dark room, I listened to Sylvia's uneven breathing. I opened my eyes, and the bedroom was the navy blue of night. She wheezed and rolled over. I ached to get up to feel her forehead but didn't want to wake her. And then I heard it.

An explosion, a crack in the night air. My senses were alert for both the sound to come again and to hear Sylvia breathe in and then out. Another crack sounded and then the rattling exhale of my child. Was it fireworks? Fireworks are common at Christmas. No light shone under the bedroom door, so I knew everyone else in the house was asleep. Another booming sound echoed. Was it something else? Behind Campo Bello, just beyond a field where cows graze, is a military base where Black Hawk helicopters take off like prehistoric birds. These monstrous modern-day dinosaurs roar to life, the sound startling until you get used to it. Crack. This didn't sound like a helicopter. I pushed thoughts of grenades and gunfire from my head. Danger was everywhere from the streets of this subdivision to the child at the foot of my bed fighting a fever.

At last the crack of explosions or fireworks faded, and I climbed out of bed, my footsteps silent on the worn carpeting. I leaned down to brush my hand lightly across her cheek. Her skin was soft but hot to the touch, its usual suppleness gone slack with illness. Sylvia wheezed again in her sleep, making a tiny mewing sound, and my heart felt as though it were made of crystal.

Parenting, I thought, even in a mountain city in Colombia, is an endless loop of pain and strength, messes and cleaning, hardship and intimacy. Its cycle spirals tighter and tighter when children are sick, when they are upset, when life's delicate balance is thrown off. It is in the ebb and flow of illness and health, happiness and fear, anger and forgiveness, that a life takes shape.

After Silas had scattered his mother's ashes in the Cauca River, a stray dog with mangy fur and wagging tail came wandering through the grass toward us, and Sylvia had clutched at me, her primal fear aroused despite the bright eyes of the creature. I had always assumed that fears, however irrational, existed to keep you safe. But now I wasn't sure. As I held Sylvia close, I could feel her heart beating with the rhythm of the river. Even as my father bent down to scratch the dog's crooked ears, my daughter whimpered in fear—an unfounded, useless fear. What, I wondered, was the purpose of being afraid?

I pressed the back of my hand against Sylvia's forehead in the cloudy dimness of the bedroom. Maybe fear did not have to be a construct of life. After all, being unafraid couldn't keep one safe. With or without fear, Beth had died, and Dave's mother had died, and no amount of anticipations or precautions could have kept them alive. We cannot change these things any more than I can change when my father revealed his secrets. The present—my father throwing a stick for a dog or my daughter wheezing with an upper respiratory illness—was reality, and fear—guerrillas in the hills above us or antibiotic-resistant strains of bacteria—might be nothing more than imagination. We can't change the present—or the past—but we can move forward, do what needs to be done. I kissed my child's fevered head and slipped back into bed.

■ ■ ■

By morning, Sylvia, her body filled with antibiotics, was ready to play video games with her cousin, and I was ready for a large cup of coffee.

"¿Cómo amaneciste, my dear?" my father asked as I came into the dining room. "How did you sleep?"

"I heard noises last night," I said, yawning. "Maybe fireworks?"

Silas took a sip of *café con leche* and exchanged looks with our dad.

"At least they sounded like fireworks," I said. A plate of eggs and *arepas* waited for me.

Silas looked away.

"You keep telling yourself that, my dear." My father laughed and drained his coffee cup.

And I wondered why he would still try to shelter me, protect me. Clearly Silas knew something about those noises, and I did not. I could feel my chest tighten in frustration—no, in anger.

"They weren't fireworks?" I said, coming out and asking the question to which I wanted the answer.

"They weren't," my father said, his smile fading a bit.

They weren't fireworks. I pushed the eggs around my plate, the yellow mounds suddenly unappetizing. Those explosive sounds in the dark of night were just as frightening as I thought they had been, no trick of the imagination. Sometimes stories are true.

I opened my mouth as if to say something. But what? Whom could I be mad at? Whose fault was the tension I felt in my stomach?

"Uncle Dave!" Santino shouted. Both children, Sylvia still pale and ghostlike, came careening around the corner of the hallway, startling the birds that were eating their own breakfast in the courtyard. "Let's go to the park!"

Dave looked at me, then at my father and my brother. "Find your shoes," he told Sylvia and Santino.

When I first arrived in Colombia more than fifteen years earlier, my father's house had been surrounded by vacant lots, and the streets had been muddy and unpaved. Now Campo Bello was crowded with two-story plaster buildings with the familiar red tile roofs. A convenience store on the corner sold candies and cigarettes, and a playground—complete with a swing set and seesaw—had been built in a small square.

"Why aren't we driving, Uncle Dave?" Santino asked as he followed Dave and me out of the house.

"Because we're walking."

"How far is it?" Sylvia whined, dragging the toes of her shoes along the asphalt.

"Around the corner, you two goofs."

When we came around the corner, the two cousins took off running. They scrambled up the climbing structure, which was made of large, even tree trunks painted in bright primary colors. A pavilion had been built at one end of the park, where now, at Christmastime, a nativity scene had been constructed. The *pesebre* represented not only Mary and Joseph and the manger but also rolling green hills, grazing animals, rock outcroppings, and chickens pecking for food. It was a diorama of Colombia in miniature. The green hills that took your breath away with their vibrancy; the mountains with such steep slopes it looked as if the vegetation itself might come loose; the small enclaves of peasants and Indians farming the land, herding the cows, chasing the poultry. When my mother had lived in Colombia, these nativity scenes had been the sole decorations for Christmas, often occupying an entire corner of a living room, she had told me. At the house, Sylvia and Santino had created their own little *pesebre*, with glue and plastic animals.

"Look at me, Uncle Dave!" shouted Santino from the top step of the slide.

"Mama, look at me!" Sylvia said from her perch on the monkey bars.

Dave and I stood on the edge of the grass, the Andean hills behind us, and watched them play and climb, swing and run. The two of them could have been brother and sister, each with sandy-brown hair and dark eyes, each with round, pale faces and quick smiles. I took Dave's hand in mine, and it felt warm and safe as I closed my eyes and let the sun beat down on my half-Colombian skin.

"What's this for?" Santino asked, and I opened my eyes.

"It's a seesaw," Dave said and told him how it worked.

"Hey, Sylvia," Santino shouted, and his cousin joined him.

The seesaw was made of thick logs and had wooden slabs attached at each end for seats. The centerpiece was painted bright red, one seat was yellow, and the other green. Each child chose a seat and climbed on, teetering and tottering as they should, with very little of Dave's help. At last they were settled and went up and down. Sylvia, the heavier of the two, quickly figured out how to kick off as she neared the ground, a motion that sent her soaring into the air. Up and down. Down and up.

These two children, born only nine days apart after decades of deceit and secrets. A boy and a girl, I marveled, who would grow up friends, cousins, who had broken the cycle of secrets. I felt a pang of regret at what could have been and imagined, for a moment, a six-year-old Silas and a six-year-old Anika playing together, going up and down on a seesaw. They are both dark haired and brown skinned, one is chubby, the other thin. The little boy runs as fast as he can, the little girl tries to keep up. They argue, perhaps over the best swing on the playground, and then perhaps they share instead, take turns. Perhaps they are siblings but are meeting each other for the first time in this country where they have never lived. Perhaps each child's mother has brought them here to have a reunion not only with one another but with a dark, mustachioed man whom everyone calls their father. He has followed them to the playground but stands off a bit, a cigarette in one hand. The two mothers watch from a distance, as well, a bit wary, probably shy. But the two children, these two little dark-haired children, don't let that bother them right now. There are swings and seesaws to explore, a bug recently found in a pile of sand, a flower blooming on an unfamiliar tree. These two children shout and laugh, a brother and sister.

"I'm done," Santino announced as he began to climb off his end of the seesaw.

"Wait," Dave and I cried in unison, cringing lest one of them get hit in the face. It was, of course, all about balance.

35

THE POPAYÁN MUNICIPAL AIRPORT is tiny, just a couple of runways and a single departure lounge. From the terminal I couldn't see the air traffic control center, the place where the men my mother had taught English to all those years before had worked. But I didn't try to imagine what did or might have or could have happened—it was more important that I was here. Dave, Sylvia, and I were leaving one day earlier than Silas and his family, so all eight of us had once again packed into the Hyundai—one child on a lap in front, four across the back seat with one more child on a lap—like a caricature of a Colombian family. We laughed and joked in half Spanish, half English all the way to the airport as Ceci made hard turns and abrupt stops.

"Where is your Colombian passport?" the woman behind the counter asked when I presented our tickets and passports. I was used to this question now, and besides, I had my father here to vouch for me. I expertly explained my situation again, and she handed back my tickets after checking our luggage.

The waiting area was big and white with white tiles and white paint on the walls, as whitewashed as the city itself. Popayán. *La ciudad blanca.* A city washed clean, repainted, always fresh and new. If an earthquake couldn't destroy it, one small family tree's roots couldn't disturb it. The children ran in circles around the rows of mostly empty white chairs.

"Ay, Anika," said Ceci in a plaintive tone, taking my hand.

It said everything we were thinking. Did these ten days really go by so quickly? Would Sylvia remember this trip? Would I be back?

Even if Spanish had been my native language, I don't think I could have expressed what I was feeling. Instead I said, "Ay, Ceci," in what I hoped was an equally plaintive voice.

A garbled announcement came over the loudspeaker, and my father stood up. "You should probably go through," he said.

And I burst into tears, tears that had, perhaps, been waiting all these years, tears that had welled in my eyes since I was a baby, a toddler, a teenager, a new parent.

He reached for me and hugged me, and I cried harder. Everything from the first phone call to the inscrutable emails to the paintings that hung on walls spilled out through my tears. My father squeezed me, strangled me with his embrace, and the sharp strap of my bag cut into my back. I lifted my head from his shoulder and saw a wet spot on his blue shirt where my tears had dampened the fabric, perhaps the same spot where I had spit up as a baby, the same spot where I had laid my downy infant head. I stepped back and looked around for my daughter. She came running and grabbed my hand in her small one as I wiped my cheeks with my sleeve.

"We'll be back," I said more forcefully than I felt. "We will. We'll be back." I had to say it out loud so that I might begin to believe it.

"Even if you don't come back," my father said, "it's okay because this has been the most beautiful thing in my life, to have my family all here together. I can die happy."

"We'll be back," I said again and bumped my shoulder against his, trying to smile widely.

The intercom mumbled again, and we gathered our things, and Sylvia's hand was held, and then, somehow, we were through the gate and beyond the door, and my family—my Colombian family—disappeared from view.

Dave and I settled into our seats with Sylvia between us once again. I held his hand across our daughter's lap as the plane took off, gripping his fingers even in the slight, completely normal turbulence of high-altitude airflow. I knew that the fact of our hurtling through air was miraculous and that my own place in this world was, like all of ours, a result of happenstance and chance and maybe even love. Perhaps, I thought, looking down at the blurred city lights through the scratched Plexiglas window, if an airplane could defy gravity, then I could defy fear and nostalgia and blame. Perhaps I could abandon what might have been for what was and what would be. As night fell and the cabin grew quiet and dim, Sylvia curled up in her seat, and I listened to the rhythmic sucking of her thumb as she drifted into sleep. I pressed my forehead against the glass and looked down to see zigzags of lightning—magic and energy—jumping from cloud to cloud, links across all the emptiness of the dark sky.

EPILOGUE

IT IS SUMMER. Strollers bite at our ankles, fat men and pregnant women bump us, and entwined couples block our progress. Sylvia tags along behind us as we wander a street fair in Minneapolis. The salty smell of corn dogs and French fries and the delicate aroma of handmade soaps and sachets of dried prairie flowers mingle with my memory of the pungent odor of *ajo* and the sweetness of *panela* in the market in Silvia high in the Andes. I think of my mother crossing streets with a protective hand over her belly, of the little Guambiano girl with her cup of coffee, of Silas and me drinking *aguardiente* in the plaza.

As I drift into the past, I catch a glimpse of a family, distorted and backward, in the window of a Starbucks. The father, tall and thin, walks in front with a long, confident gait. He grips the hand of a black-haired woman in a purple sundress and large sunglasses. The blur of a little girl in pink sandals trails behind them, skipping and twirling, wisps of toffee-colored hair escaping her braid. She grabs hold of the woman's sash every few feet before letting it go.

And then I see that this family—this mismatched triad reflected in the glass—is my family. My husband. My daughter. Me. This family of mine shimmers, our images superimposed over the queue of people inside. Dave and I have been together for a lifetime, and this little brown-haired girl is still a blip on the time line of our lives. But this is all it takes, I realize, to make a family: love, blood, time.

When I was a child, I used to blur my vision by squinting my eyes at something close but letting my focus drift far away. Everything would become hazy and gauzy, mystical and strange. I preferred to look at the world like this, this backward, unfocused view. I liked to observe the everyday from another perspective or to imagine what didn't happen, what couldn't, what could have. Blurring my vision could make strange things look safe and the known feel exciting.

For a split second the reflection of a little boy seems to appear in the glass and then fades. I don't know who is inside and who is outside, who is a mirage and who is real. Our reflections—these shapes and shadows that make up my family—in the window of the coffee shop look like strangers until I look again, and like magic, our images shift and sharpen, and the three of us in the glass are as intimate as my own skin. I close my eyes for an instant, and in the darkness behind my lids I realize that these figures could be—in a different light, a different moment, a different place or space—my own once-upon-a-time family, my family that never was, me as daughter instead of mother. Time stands still, and time flips and flows. When I open my eyes again and look at the reflection, I see.

ACKNOWLEDGMENTS

MAGICAL REALISM FOR NON-BELIEVERS would not exist without the support of my family, friends, and community. Thank you to my editor at the University of Minnesota Press, Erik Anderson, for believing that my words could become this book and for the magic worked by my lovely agent, Thao Le.

Thanks to the Loft Literary Center in Minneapolis, where I took my first writing class, and to the 2009–10 Mentor Series, through which I met the community of writers that changed my life. Thank you to mentors Shannon Olson, Pablo Medina, and JC Hallman, who helped me figure out what I didn't know and what I did. Special thanks to mentor Dinah Lenney for giving feedback and including "What Didn't Happen" in *Brief Encounters: A Collection of Contemporary Creative Nonfiction.*

Minnesota's support of artists through the Artist Initiative Grants makes the winters here almost bearable. Thanks to the Minnesota State Arts Board and to the Jerome Foundation for generous grants. Thanks also to the literary magazines that first published essays that eventually became part of this book, especially *Hippocampus Magazine* and *Apt Literary Magazine* for publishing multiple pieces along the way.

Before the editors and agents, grants and magazines, there were many hours of writing and the support of friends. Thank you, Karlyn Coleman, for keeping me going—and for enabling my coffee habit. I am especially grateful to Fred Amram and Mary Jane LaVigne for their unflinchingly honest critiques that helped make me a better writer. And thanks to early readers and supporters Laura Randgaard and Amber Larson.

A memoir of finding family owes a lot to those who let me share their stories. Thank you to my mom, who raised me to be my own person (and who is a wonderful grandmother to Sylvia); to my dad, who sees me as an artist; and to my grandparents, who first taught me that books contain worlds, stories, and sometimes even answers. Thanks also to Milenka Idrogo, Santino Saunders, María Cecilia Paredes, Melinda Smith, and my Colombian *primos* and *tías*. And I am grateful for the magic and reality that gave me the best brother a sister could hope for.

Of course, thank you to my two favorite people in the world: my amazing and unique daughter, Sylvia Dieken, the reason I get out of bed every day, and Dave, who has been there for me the whole time.

ANIKA FAJARDO was born in Colombia and raised in Minnesota. Her writing has been published in the anthologies *Brief Encounters: A Collection of Contemporary Nonfiction*; *Love and Profanity: A Collection of True, Tortured, Wild, Hilarious, Concise, and Intense Tales of Teenage Life*; and *Sky Blue Water: Great Stories for Young Readers* (Minnesota, 2016). She has received awards from the Jerome Foundation, the Minnesota State Arts Board, and the Loft Literary Center. She lives with her husband and daughter in Minneapolis.